THE
WINTER FLOWER GARDEN

THE WINTER FLOWER GARDEN

SONIA KINAHAN

The
Leisure
Circle

For John
who loved winter flowers and made the garden with me

© 1985 Sonia Kinahan
Line illustrations by Mike Dodd

This edition specially produced for The Leisure Circle Limited by
Croom Helm Ltd, Provident House, Burrell Row, Beckenham, Kent BR3 1AT
Croom Helm Australia Pty Ltd, Suite 4, 6th Floor, 64-76 Kippax Street,
Surry Hills, NSW 2010, Australia

Kinahan, Sonia
    The winter flower garden.
    1. Plants, Ornamental — Great Britain
    2. Winter gardening
    I. Title
    635.9'53   SB406

    ISBN 0-7099-1560-8

Typeset by Leaper & Gard Ltd, Bristol, England
Printed and bound in Great Britain

Contents

Colour Plates

Figures

Acknowledgements

I would like to thank those many friends and relatives who have given me both encouragement and help during the writing of this book; and my three daughters, Deirdre, Vanessa and Melanie, particularly, for their additional aid in checking, proof-reading and indexing. To my dear friends Christopher Hibbert, Marian Babson, and the late Joyce Weiner, for their wise counsel and practical support. Also to the following for their advice on specific points concerning the often controversial nomenclature of plants and their spelling: Miss Rosemary Angel of the Museums Division, Kew Gardens; Dr Brent Elliott, the Librarian of the Royal Horticultural Society's Lindley Library; Mr Christopher Lloyd, the expert and writer on gardens; and Mr John Kelly of the Abbotsbury Gardens. And to the staff of the Hastings Public Library for their indulgence and courteous help.

The basic photographic illustrations are mine, taken in the garden, but I am obliged to *Homes and Gardens* magazine for four colour pictures of my flowers; and to Michael Warren for several more, chiefly the black and white. The book jacket photograph of me was taken by Mark Summers at the time of the filming of the television programme 'Gardeners' World'.

Finally my special thanks to Mike Dodd for the jacket illustration and black and white line drawings, which convey exactly the effect I wanted, to illustrate the beautiful flowers of winter.

Sonia Kinahan,
Sandes House,
St Leonards-on-Sea,
Sussex

Introduction

Winter is a time when we especially need colour and pleasure to make our journey through the colder half of the year more enjoyable. I have found that plants flowering in the garden play an important part in this, coupled with the soft or vibrant colour of their blooms and the agreeable perfume that so many of them possess and with which they scent the garden.

I have not been able to find a book that is entirely devoted to winter flowers. Several books have been written on winter colour, but these always include with the flowers, coloured barks, leaves and berries; and these, to my mind, are a poor exchange for real flowers, with their lovely scent.

I count my winter span from 15 November to 15 March for convenience, though the seasons don't run true to form every year, a cold early spring sometimes delaying the last of the winter-flowering plants till well into April. Then the first real warmth brings a rush of plants blooming all together with the next season's, making a real show. But luckily a warm early spring spreads the flowering nicely, as the winter flowers come through to greet the spring blooms.

When planning the winter garden I try to position the flowering plants so that they can be seen from the various windows of the house, should the weather be too unpleasant to venture out. And I try to concentrate the most highly-scented ones near the back and front doors, so that as soon as you open up, to let visitors in, or animals out, you get the benefit of a waft of fragrance from a nearby daphne, *Daphne odora*, or a honeysuckle, *Lonicera fragrantissima*. For some reason winter flowers seem to be more highly scented on average than blooms in the other parts of the year. Perhaps to help pollination.

I believe it is always possible to have some flowers every day of the year, with careful regard for the vagaries of whatever climate you live in. It may be that a disastrous gale or heavy fall of snow will make this difficult, but I try to have some plants in pots, so that they can be carried in to the protection of a greenhouse or sunny porch, away from the temporary inclemency of the weather which is attempting to break and destroy the newly-opened flower branches. When the shrub is too big or firmly planted in the soil, then some form of protection must be the solution. Binding the stem of a tree with felt will stop the bark being split by frost, particularly when there has been warm damp weather, which keeps the sap rising, for when a sudden cold snap comes, the soft fleshy stem is more vulnerable to being split by frost. But, on the other hand, with a gradual dropping of temperature and dry conditions, the plant becomes more acclimatised. The top part of the tree or shrub may be damaged by the frost and particularly a dry cold wind, but the covering of felt will enable the base of the stem to survive and with any luck this will sprout again next spring.

For the protection of smaller plants the simplest way is with a box, either of cardboard or wood, placed over the plant and held down with a large stone or brick for a few days while the tormenting weather lasts. Rain coming to wet the box usually means a rise in temperature, so the stone can quickly be removed before the box, if cardboard, collapses on to your choice plant. These boxes can then be discarded and a new one used next time. I have found this a fairly labour-saving way to bring my tender winter flowers through the worst patches of weather, and even if the edges of the plant are scorched, the main root will have been saved to flower another day.

I have not described every possible plant in all details, as these can be found in any good gardening reference book or comprehensive catalogue. I list only the ones I know, have growing, or would like to have growing in my garden. My aim is to explain why I am so fascinated by the idea of trying to bring colour of flower and scent into the winter, and to describe those which I have found work best to do this for me. Of the roughly one hundred species I discuss plus their varieties, I like to rely on having about twenty-five of these in flower in any one month. So that over four full months — one divided into the last half of November and the first half of March, when there is always much more bloom anyway with the over-lapping of autumn and spring flowers — I should have seen at least one hundred different flowers cheering the winter scene.

I first began to think about the position of the garden in winter when I noticed so many articles telling me to pull up all the summer bedding plants and clear the beds and dig them over and cut everything down and make all ready for spring sowing. I could not bear to discard plants still giving flower, so I always left them, anyway, to carry on until the frosts did their worst, and in a mild winter an annual against a wall on the south side of the house will survive quite happily. I have had a *Gazania splendens* for several years now in such a protected position and it flowers all the year round, suitably encouraged by dead-heading, whereas in the border in the main part of the garden, the first frosts will carry it off. In a cold year or with prolonged frost I box it over and take cuttings, but usually the heart of the plant survives.

So I decided to be adventurous and see what could be grown in the way of larger shrubs and trees. Gradually the numbers increased, and although I regularly lose one or two plants through cold or dryness or wind or excessive wetness, the return has been well worth the small loss, which can be ameliorated in any case, if I remember to take cuttings of delicate and vulnerable types. So bare beds and rockeries have been avoided and I am saved from ending up with the garden clear and only the much overrated double-digging to perform — invented years ago, incidentally, to give the hordes of gardeners employed on big estates something to do when the beds were emptied for the winter. Many more plants, such as camellias, were grown in greenhouses or stove-houses in those days before it was realised they were perfectly hardy out of doors. And why sit in an armchair reading catalogues of spring and summer flowers, when a corner could be found for a scented bloom to enjoy at that very moment.

So I would encourage anyone who wants to take a chance too, to go and see some of these plants, growing in famous gardens and public parks, or in Botanic gardens and their glasshouses. Also, in the better, sometimes smaller, nurseries whose owners are themselves really interested in cultivating, or able and willing to get a special request for you. Then have a stab at growing it outdoors yourself and select a suitable spot very carefully, giving extra protection if the garden is in an area noted for cold winters. In this case a wall, a hedge, an overhanging tree branch or a sunken site will all make a few degrees difference; or choose to plant it in a large pot, big enough to let it develop properly, but not so heavy that you can't carry it out of the wind or under cover of some kind when a storm threatens to blow it over, or bitter cold is forecast, so severe that the root in the pot will be in danger of freezing solid. The latter, of course, can be tempered by covering the soil in the pot with extra leaf-mould or compost, but there are still the sides at risk, so pots are always more vulnerable in this way — with certain plants, particularly. For instance, camellias will suffer, but not rhododendrons.

The plants I discuss in the various chapter months are an arbitrary and personal selection in that not only do they vary in flowering time according to the particular weather in any one winter, but also according to the part of the country they are grown in and the position they have been planted in in the garden; each one of these factors making a considerable difference to the end result.

Obviously in a cold situation they will flower a few weeks later; even so, many are still perfectly hardy. But if you cannot get them to survive and still want the pleasure of a particular flowering plant, then the greenhouse will have to be resorted to. I have not taken greenhouse cultivation into account in this book, as I feel it is a confession of failure in this context, though I do have and use a cold glasshouse to shelter my summer geranium pots and grow seedlings and cuttings. And where, incidentally, I have been forced to house my two oleandar plants, which, however good the summer, will not flower successfully for me outside. Now they are trees grown into the floor soil and need heavy pruning each year so that I can get inside the place to use it for potting.

Maybe there will be failures outside, as I have often had. But success is frequent enough to make it all worthwhile and it does bring cheer to lighten the spirits during the depressing short days. In fact, so busy have I been, that before I realise it, spring has arrived, to me an often disappointing time of the year; it always seems to be colder and wetter and bleaker in the lengthening hours of daylight than I had hoped for. No, give me winter or high summer or autumn in the garden any time. As the saying is, spring can be a little late this year; and I have found this to be true, and too painfully often.

To get the most benefit from the flowers of winter, I have evolved several ways of minimising the adverse effects when a climate is not the ideal that the plant is used to. I group my shrubs fairly close together, nearer than the distance advised by the experts, so that they give protection to each other, from wind as much as the cold, and I site them also near walls or hedges for extra warmth. With many species there are varieties which are miniature — trees have half-standards, for instance — and the nearer the ground they are, the less force they have to stand from the wind, and small plants can be covered by a box and brought through a bitter spell so much more easily. Then if the plant is of the herbaceous type or one that needs hard pruning, I leave the spent stems and foliage and don't cut them off and tidy up too early; this apparent mess will protect the tender shoots near the ground and bring them through the frost. My fuchsias always come through the winter protected in this way only. If everyone advises you that a particular plant is too tender for your area, take a chance and try and confound them by expending effort and thought on the position and shelter you give it, but take cuttings before the cold arrives, so that, should the worst happen, you have little plants to carry on and perhaps give success another year.

But the most important dividend from your flowers in winter is to be able to see them at all times, rain or shine, whenever you take a look out of the windows; but just occasionally you can have a plant tucked away round a corner, so that there is a surprise when walking round. And never forget to group a selection of fragrant shrubs near the back and front doors, so that if the weather should prove too bad to walk round the garden, these are accessible and you can still appreciate your scented flowers to the full. And I think this all helps to keep the potential drabness of winter at bay.

By planting shrubs closely together you also achieve a nicely massed effect when they flower. And this I have found to be a good idea, for another reason, when the climate is colder than they are used to. Mediterranean plants grow quickly in the hot sun and a few plants will soon give a massed effect in a flowerbed or cascading down a cliff wall. But in cooler and less sunny climes every process is slowed down and to get the result you want in the flowering time of the plant, having them near each other achieves somewhere near the same result as in their native situation. Many years ago a very knowledgeable man came and helped us in the garden for a while, as he had retired from a famous nursery where he had been in charge. He didn't prune shrubs very hard but let them grow naturally so that one supported the other and so protected it. This gave a very nice natural effect to the beds, but I find now that with very mature well-grown trees and shrubs, judicious pruning to keep their shape, and stop them grabbing too much light and moisture from each other, is a necessary and desirable way to keep the garden in fair order, leaving some spontaneous effect, but giving all of them an equal chance to show off their flowers when the time comes.

Where possible, the ground below and around the bigger trees and shrubs can be planted with smaller alpines and bulbs that do not mind the shade and like the protection given from above. These will form clumps and make drifts of plantings and in time will be very labour-saving as ground cover — a very high priority in the present day when most people have to manage their gardens without additional help. In my garden of just half an acre, where thirty years ago we had a gardener one whole day a week, I now manage on my own with occasional help in summer with the mowing of the lawns and any task too heavy to tackle alone. This is made possible because I do not have elaborate bedding out of plants in the summer (cleared away so ruthlessly by gardeners in the past at the first sign of autumn), and I keep some of the odd corners of the garden rather wild so that plants like nettles can grow for butterflies, which in winter hibernate in the ivies that I now let clothe some of the border trees.

I find it necessary to lighten my solid clay soil, which is still so heavy in some places you could model with it, in spite of thirty years of adding compost and peat and forest bark. But in the better parts of the garden I grow my special plants and with the liberal mixture of leaf-mould and acid compost I find I can grow my camellias and rhododendrons fairly successfully. I believe they are slower to reach their full size in the not-ideal soil, but they do not seem to be slow to flower very freely, which is what I want.

So on 15 November I look out for my first winter flower. Of course, if the autumn is fine, many of the summer-flowering plants will still be in full bloom, especially if I have been watchful in cutting off all the spent heads as soon as they are 'blown' as an old gardener acquaintance of mine used to call the dying of the flowers.

In my search for a book that deals with flowers in winter only, I have come across several that include coloured barks, leaves and berries, things which I have to admit are anathema to me. I know this is a very personal view and that the berries are a bonus for the birds, but all these extras are a poor exchange for real flowers, often scented, and I do not count them in or think they are any more worth considering than as a background, like the soil, the grass and the clouds in the sky. They all add to the general picture in the garden, but this is brought alive and transformed by the flowers.

How To Use This Book

The Chart

This book is based on my personal experiences of gardening near the coast in an area basically of Zone Temperature 6, and of how I manage to grow plants beyond my own zone (from 5-7) by the application of various methods — planting in moist or well-drained soil; on the right site, from an aspect sloping towards the south and the sun, to a cold northerly position in shade; by the use of walls for extra warmth or wind protection and even covers for small plants or stem-wrapping for larger ones. Certain plants will stand frozen ground, and bloom, despite any harsh conditions, the flowers appearing through deep snow. Others require a considerable thickness of mulch to protect their roots from heavy frost and then they will survive, even though their foliage is affected. But where winters are very severe, with prolonged periods of deep snow, or low temperatures resulting in solidly frozen ground, glasshouse protection, even heated, may be necessary to preserve the plants and produce the flowering. Even this is very well worthwhile, for the pleasure of being able to go into a greenhouse, or small conservatory attached to the house, or even a small glasshouse on an apartment balcony window, and to see a few flowers you have grown, in however little a container, and enjoy their sweet scent — while beyond your enclosure, the snow lies deep, the cold wind blows, and the ground is frozen for possibly many weeks.

In the chart at the end of this book I give the ideal conditions in which a plant has been found to grow best. So whenever I mention a plant in the text, referral to this chart will give anyone intending to grow it, wherever they may live and in whatever part of the world, an idea of the exact requirements and the temperature zones it can tolerate.

For example *Abelia grandiflora*, the first entry, of unknown origin, is a shrub, evergreen, which will reach a maximum height of 6 ft, and a spread of 3 ft sq, with flowers of white/pink blooming from July to November, which should be planted in April in neutral soil in a sunny position, sheltered as it is tender. The pruning it needs is shaping and the removal of dead wood, and it can be propagated by taking a cutting in July. It will tolerate the temperatures and conditions of Zones 6 and 7, and is more fully described in Chapters 1 and 7, and the flowers are faintly scented.

But these requirements can be reproduced to a certain extent by the application of the methods I suggest, bearing in mind that the plant will always develop more successfully if given the site, soil and moisture it likes. Nevertheless, these can be provided with some thought and preparation, and many plants are surprisingly adaptable and make the most of the conditions they find themselves in, as long as they are not asked to survive in ones too extreme from those to which they have become acclimatised, in their natural habitat. For instance, in desert conditions, a shade and moisture-loving plant must obviously be shaded and watered with care; and an alpine, such as one of the saxifrages, liking gritty well-drained soil, must have a heavy soggy position considerably lightened. In the high alpine regions it endures very cold dry conditions, and warmer moister areas, though apparently more amenable, will cause it to damp off. So these types of plants are often grown on grit in a glasshouse, where light and air can be manually controlled.

The Maps

By referring to the maps at the end of the book which show the various zones in different parts of the world, it is possible to estimate quite easily whether a plant mentioned as being able to tolerate a particular temperature zone will grow in the area in which you are intending to plant it. As mentioned before, the shelter and position you give each plant must be allowed for and will give greater scope; and in the southern hemisphere, obviously, the months must be adjusted and fitted to those in the northern winter ones. Other factors, such as the type of ground and the amount of rainfall available will also affect the rate of growth and time of flowering to a certain extent, although these can be adjusted by planting in suitable soil or by mixing up the special needs of a particular plant, like peat for acid-lovers, and adding this to the available ground. Dry conditions, too, can be changed by adequate watering and wet heavy clay can be lightened by the addition of sand, peat and friable humus. The one element you have no control over is the climate, and even this you can only estimate, as in the best of zones it will vary slightly each year from the norm, and in others the variation can be quite dramatic. But if you are ready and prepared to tackle whatever comes, I find it amazing how, in most winters, successful flowers can be produced.

Chapter 1

November

The fifteenth of November can be mild or cold, clear or foggy, but whatever it is like, the time for winter flowers has begun. So much depends on the weather as to what will be in bloom on this first day. But if the winter flowers are late, there are always plenty of autumn-flowering ones which go on well into winter and bridge any gap caused by unreasonable climate for that particular year.

I have a twenty-five-year-old bush of *Viburnum × bodnantense* which is now tree-size, being more than 12 ft high and this produces several flowers, hidden among its leaves, as early as August. By October it is fully in bloom and as the frost comes and the leaves drop, the full beauty of the flower clusters of sweetly-scented pink buds opening to velvety white little trumpet blooms is revealed. And these go on appearing all through the winter months and their strong perfume will drench a room with their fragrance. Two slightly different clones of this lovely viburnum have since been introduced, 'Dawn' and then 'Deben', where the buds and flowers are often both white. It takes a very severe frost to damage the blooms of any of these, though they brown slightly as they age and die. *V. farreri (fragrans)* is also of similar habit, but can fail to flower in a hard winter.

Another long-flowering winter treasure is the Autumn Cherry, *Prunus subhirtella* 'Autumnalis'. Again it may produce a few flowers tucked among the leaves, before these drop for the winter. But the special beauty and value of this tree is the frequency with which it covers its bare branches in palest pink blossoms. A few warm days or a sunny spell and the buds open out. In a cold snap the flowers are browned, but the waiting buds refuse to unfurl and stay sensibly closed until the weather improves. The variety *P. subhirtella* 'Autumnalis Rosea' has semi-double flowers of a slightly stronger pink.

T.C. Mansfield says of eucryphia, in the shrub edition of my favourite set of reference books, 'it is a shrub to covet, to cajole and to cosset'. My

Figure 1.1: *Viburnum* × *bodnantense*

Figure 1.2: *Prunus subhirtella* 'Autumnalis'

eucryphia, which is now a tall slim graceful tree, starts flowering in August. It is the variety *E. × intermedia*, a cross between *E. glutinosa* and *E. lucida* and the cup-shaped flowers are white with dark purple anthers and these clothe the branches among the glossy, slightly sticky evergreen leaves. I find that in my garden the flowering continues well into November and in a mild period will go on to Christmas, till the delicate flowers are browned by frost. But it is a sight to see this columnar tree covered with its distinctive blossoms. They prefer an acid or neutral soil, but mine has survived and grown to some 12 ft in heavy clay, protected from the worst weather by surrounding rowan and philadelphus trees, but not overhung by them, so that the soil has a chance to dry out. There is also a gradual slope in this part of the garden so good drainage may have persuaded it to ignore the unsuitable loam, and it shows how you can get away with adverse conditions and still produce a reasonable plant. I believe it is always worth having a try. Before I knew anything about what you can and cannot grow in any one area I bought various azaleas from that original chain store and planted them in the rockery. They still flower well after many many years. I imagine they found a pocket of soil between the rocks which had been broken up and proved friable enough to accommodate the fine roots of this group of shrubs. Now that I know a little more about the needs of plants, I wouldn't dare put most rhododendrons and azaleas straight into my clay without special preparation, and I tend to opt out by giving the winter-flowering ones I particularly want to grow an ericaceous proprietary mixture in large clay pots.

It is difficult to say when the tree ceanothus *C. arboreus* 'Trewithen Blue' comes into flower, for it never seems to be without some sprays of bloom. Unlike most of the other ceanothus species and their hybrids, it has large panicles like lilac flowers and of an intense blue, fading as they age; and this form is evergreen and well worth trying in a sheltered place, in a corner or against a wall; though my tree is free-standing in full sunshine, but towards the bottom of the garden, protected to some degree from the prevailing wind and in a position where I hope the frost will slip by, down the slight incline. I gather from talking to a nurseryman that this is a difficult tree to grow where the conditions are very lush and therefore wet and it does better on a poor, stony well-drained soil.

The ceanothus are known as the Californian Lilacs and I think this one really lives up to its name. A specimen growing at the end of a small town garden which I know is a continual delight to everyone living around, for after ten years its trunk is 8 in across, the reach of the branches 20 ft sq and its continuous flowering attracts comment and interest from all who see it.

Another decorative tree that reaches its peak of flowering in November is *Arbutus unedo*. It will grow in great hedges in any mild area and in the South of France I have seen great trees massed along the roadside. It is always a pleasant shrub to have in the garden as the glossy evergreen leaves make a good foil for other plants. In the autumn the clusters of

Figure 1.3: *Eucryphia* × *intermedia*

white pitcher-like flowers come into bloom and the fruits from the previous year's flowering, having remained on the tree, gradually develop into strawberry-textured balls, which are at first yellow, then turn orange and finally ripen to a deep red. So that at any one time, the tree is a mixture of white flowers and the three different colours of slowly ripening fruits. These fruits are edible and in Corsica are used to make a kind of jam. *A. unedo* 'Rubra' is a heavy cropper with glossy pink flowers. *A menziesii*, known as the 'Madrona' of California, is from western North America, but does not flower until the spring.

Although it is a slightly tender plant, my tree grows exposed to the westerly gales and stands up to them very well, despite the loss of a complete limb one year in a Force 9 battering. But it has now redressed its lop-sided appearance and is 10 ft sq. There is a Grecian variety of this so-called Killarney Strawberry Tree named *A. andrachne*, and a fine cross between these two, known as *A. × andrachnoides* where the rich brown bark is strikingly tinged with red. This is reasonably hardy and although these arbutus trees grow larger in ericaceous soils, they are surprisingly lime-tolerant. Certainly mine seems completely happy in my heavy clay ground, albeit in a well-drained position.

A shrub with a really intense blue flower and strangely prickly hairs on its red stems is *Ceratostigma willmottianum*. I grow it against the white wall on the south side of the house and with this protection it prolongs its flowering time from August until past November. The butterflies love this plant, toasting themselves against the sunny wall. It fits very neatly under a window as it remains around 2 ft sq, as I prune the stems to within an inch or so of the ground every spring and it makes a nice mound by flowering time. The unopened bunches of flower-buds are copper-red and the rich green leaves also become tinged with red. I think it is one of the nicest small plants to have, as the colouring is so striking and unusual.

Before November begins, the beautiful *Mahonia lomariifolia* is in full bloom. It has the largest and most flamboyant of the mahonia flowers, and the upright sticks of solid yellow, consisting of over two hundred flowers, appear in groups from the centre of the sprays of handsome but very prickly leaves. From a distance a child once thought my 8 ft bush was a banana tree, the flowers being the exact colour. It is reputed to be a tender variety, but I have not found it so, except that the large blooms and leaves need to be tied securely in a strong wind to avoid damage. But I think the time has come to prune my bush to give it a broader and stronger base and, according to the garden specialist Christopher Lloyd, you can be quite ruthless with successful results.

A strange and potentially lethal plant which I have growing at the bottom of my garden is the plant *Colletia cruciata*; originally from Uruguay and uncommon, it can, nevertheless, be obtained from specialist nurseries. The branches consist of triangular fleshy sections with fearful spines, which remain very sharp even when they have broken off and been dead and dried for some time. I have to keep this shrub, which would grow into around an 8 ft tree, very well pruned so that anyone in the garden, particularly an unsuspecting child, does not get damaged by the spines. Leaves, when they do appear, are hardly noticeable. But I hesitate to remove this intriguing plant as it is so unusual and does have little white flowers with a sweet almond scent and purple marks inside the lily-of-the-valley-shaped blossoms. *C. armata*, from Chile, has rounded spines and is slightly less spiky in appearance. It will tolerate any type of soil, but does need a warm sunny site. The safest place for these shrubs is towards the back of a sunny border, so that there is no chance of anyone accidentally touching the damaging thorns, and then the lovely winter scent can drift about for people to enjoy in safety!

The escallonias are a very desirable group of shrubs to have, particularly if you live near the sea as I do, for the glossy and sticky aromatic leaves seem to withstand the salt in the air and on the wind, and really thrive in the moist briny conditions. They are adaptable as to soil requirements and cuttings will root easily if put straight in the ground. They make a very good hedge and can be close clipped as they do not mind hard pruning. Some research found that in very exposed conditions not only do they stand up very well to fierce winds, but that if pruned in early summer after a spring flowering, they will often flower again in the autumn. Most of the varieties are shades of pink to deep red, both flower and leaf varying in size, but all of modest proportions. But one I have grown and found very vigorous is a cross between *E. montevidensis* (*bifida*) and *E. exoniensis* called *E.* 'Iveyi' with very shiny good-sized leaves and a mop of pure white flowers which are at least four to six times larger than any of the other kinds. Recently, I came across a fine tree of this plant some 30 ft high, though I have pruned my plant heavily to keep it within bounds in the border and it is barely 6 ft. Now I shall leave it to grow tall and upright, only cutting the side shoots which grow too vigorously into other surrounding shrubs. However, these will give it some protection on its lower regions, should the weather turn nasty, for *E.* 'Iveyi' is a slightly tender variety. It begins to flower in the autumn and keeps going for many weeks and the very dark green leaves make an excellent foil for the paler large leathery leaves of a spring-flowering *Clematis armandii* 'Apple Blossom' which drapes itself all over it.

Many roses can be enjoyed during the winter-flowering period, but it is essential to keep the plants dead-headed from when they first bloom in the summer, so that new shoots are continuously being produced and the energy does not go to making the bright red hips, delightful as they are on some of the plants. I have a pergola stretching across my terrace and the rambler (wichuraiana) rose *R.* 'Alberic Barbier' will go on flowering, often up till the end of the year, producing its clusters of yellow buds opening to double white flowers. The leaves of this rose are a lovely moss-green and very shiny. And two more of my favourite roses, which will often give me flowers for my Christmas table, are the Bourbon R. 'Madame Isaac Pereire' with its large heavily-scented madder-crimson blooms, and a fairly new cluster-flowered floribunda bush rose R. 'Margaret Merril' which is pure white with a mass of crimson anthers and a delicious scent. This one, particularly, lasts very well when cut for the house.

Coronilla glauca is a shrub member of the pea family. It is evergreen and has soft greyish-blue leaves and clusters of bright chrome-yellow flowers. In mild districts it will bloom all the year round, but I find with me it will rest for a few weeks in the late summer. But by October it is off again and although a tender plant, if it can be sited correctly, with its back to a warm wall and other shrubs on either side, it will withstand quite severe conditions. When snow is forecast I cover the delicate evergreen foliage with a net, so that I can lift off a heavy fall of snowflakes, which might break the branches with their weight. On shrubs with tougher branches and leaves I use a broom to knock the snow away. Of course the snow does keep the plant warm in a bitter spell, so if the fall is light I leave it alone to protect and keep the shrub cosy and away from any air frost. The situation has to be judged with some care and entails checking what weather is to be expected. But I think it is all worthwhile if I can bring a tender plant through a bad patch, even though it may lose a limb or two, or have its top-hamper browned and be forced to break from the base again.

Near the coronilla bed my rockery meets the bay window of the house and among these rocks several pink winter flowers of varying form and shade begin to bloom during the next few weeks. In fact, the little shrub *Abelia schumannii* has been dressed with its delicate sugar-pink bells for some time, with the green and bronzy leaves making such a good complement among them. In another part of the garden I have *A. × grandiflora* which is taller growing and, as its name indicates, has larger flowers. The leaves are dark green and unlike the *A. schumannii* this variety is evergreen and the flowers are white, flushed with pink, so these two plants give quite a different colour effect.

Below the abelia, tucked against the wall of the house is a group of nerine (delightfully named after a princess of Grecian mythology). I planted several *N. bowdenii* and these South African bulbs never fail to put up a foot high stem on the top of which rich pink lily-like flowers, borne in umbels, bloom in late autumn. There are varieties with various shades of pink, a pure white one and the red *N. sarniensis*, known as the Guernsey Lily, with the variety *corusca* being a brilliant orange, but not so hardy as the others; so I am starting this orange one in a pot, and can then move it about for protection depending on the weather. But as there were two little bulblet offshoots on the main bulb which I had bought, I pulled them off and now have three, all shooting in their pots. I think I shall try and plant one bulb from a pot out in a very sheltered place, where the sun will keep it warm and it will get reflected and delayed heat from a wall.

In front of these, about twenty years ago, I planted some bulbs of the

Figure 1.4: *Abelia × grandiflora*

Belladonna Lily, *Amaryllis belladonna*, and every year the leaves appeared but never the flowers, which should follow when the leaves have died down. Then three or four years ago a couple of thick stems shot up about 3 ft high and there were the beautiful baby-pink flowers, making a good contrast to the more spidery deeper-coloured nerine and the tiny shell-pink trumpets on the abelia bush. And being between stones in the rockery and the wall of the house, they are all at different levels despite their height. So they can be seen easily from various windows.

A winter-flowering herb is the Pineapple Sage, *Salvia rutilans*. It probably comes from Mexico and the hairy elliptic leaves do really smell strongly of pineapple when crushed, and can be used in salads or for flavouring sponge cakes or scenting bowls of *pot pourri*. The shrub grows very fast and, on the end of long shoots, produces 4 in scarlet racemes. It is cut down to the ground in a cold winter, but to guard against this I take cuttings which root so easily. Pieces put in water will grow a root in a few days, so I risk the main plant against a sunny southern wall and box it in bitter weather, and rely on the cuttings to continue the stock. They will come quite safely through the winter in a cold greenhouse and flower for a long time. The only drawback this salvia has is that the branches are very brittle and snap off if nudged, which is easy to do as it will reach 4 ft sq quite quickly, and therefore takes up quite a bit of room in a confined space.

Veronicas are now known as hebes, which I think is a far less romantic-sounding name, despite the fact that it has a youthful meaning. H. 'Autumn Glory' is a hardy variety and has sprays of deep violet flowers among the bronzy elliptical leaves. In fact the leaves are green and the stems aubergine-coloured, giving the general effect of a purple-foliaged bush. It makes a loose-growing little shrub and with me sprawls rather untidily but attractively over rocks. It comes into bloom as early as July and will carry on well into the new year, if the spent flower-heads are removed, so that it doesn't put all its energy into nourishing the seed heads. But among the many veronicas there is a group named H. speciosa which grows to about 5 ft sq and makes a fine sight in a mild winter, when the soft grass-green leaves and 4 in sprays of flowers are not damaged by frost. I have a hedge of one of the speciosa hybrids H. speciosa 'Alicia Amherst' which stands up to and seems quite happy with the sea winds. Most of the veronicas or hebes come from New Zealand so they are used to tolerating the salty air in those islands. As the leaves are so fleshy they will not stand a very dry cold position and like a protected corner, where, even if burnt by cold, they can be pruned down to sound wood in the spring and will, if the stems haven't been burst by frost, shoot again and soon regain their shape. There is a deep crimson H. speciosa 'Simon Delaux' and H. speciosa 'La Seduisante' another shade of rich pink, and a favourite colour of mine. They are happy in any soil and will grow under trees, though, with the lack of sun, the flowers come rather bleached.

Another bush which is in bloom nearly all the year if kept shaped and the spent flower-heads removed, is H. 'Bowles' Hybrid'. The leaves are much smaller than the speciosa type, even smaller than the 'Autumn Glory' but the stems are not so purple-tinged as the latter and the blooms are a lighter mauve and more slender in shape. I grow it in full sun but near a wall and protected on the windward side by a large prunus tree, and from the north wind by the house. And in this situation it rewards me with this mauve cloud of flower, so eye-catching whenever I look out of the window or pass by the bed.

A surprisingly hardy little bush is the dwarf variety of the myrtle, Myrtus communis tarentina. The slim glossy leaves are a tenth of the size of M. communis itself, and believing it to be in need of shelter, I planted it with its back to a warm brick wall facing south, but with the rockery falling away in front of it. The bush has now grown about 6 ft sq over and up on to the drive and into a totally exposed position, both to the prevailing westerly winds and any dry north air. Certainly the smallness of the leaves helps it to stand up to any inclement weather more successfully, but I suppose one day it may succumb. Meanwhile, from July onwards, and well into December, it is covered with red little bud balls which open out into a tiny bunch of spice-scented creamy white flowers. And the leaves are very aromatic when crushed too.

The Kaffir Lily or Crimson Flag, *Schizostylis coccinea*, grows about 2 ft tall and is very hardy, preferring a light neutral soil. The leaves are lily-like but the sprays of starry flowers — they look like a miniature gladiolus — are a striking bright red. *S. coccinea* begins to flower in August, but carries on into November when *S.* 'November Pink' take over, to be followed in December by the salmon-coloured *S.* 'Mrs Hegarty' and finally *S.* 'Viscountess Byng' which is rose-pink and the last to flower. There is a variety *S. coccinea* 'Major' which has larger flowers than all the others, but I have not grown this. These plants need a position in the garden where the sun can bake the roots, but they do not like to be very dry. In South Africa they thrive on the banks of rivers but fully exposed to the hot sun.

Sternbergia lutea and the more prolific *S. angustifolia* prefer to be grown on a chalky soil and take time to get established, for again, like many bulbs, they want a good summer bake by the sun before they will produce their chrome-yellow flowers, which are like a large crocus in form, and followed by the thong-like green leaves. Even then it is some years before they do well. They are a member of the amaryllis family and named after the German botanist Count Sternberg, though they hail from the eastern Mediterranean. *S. macrantha*, now known as *S. clusiana*, has even larger flowers like a fat yellow tulip, again blooming before glaucous leaves appear and continuing well into December.

The colour of the gentian from western China, *Gentiana sino-ornata*, is one of the best blues to have in the garden. But it likes an acid soil and plenty of moisture, so I find it is worth having a special place for it; perhaps a trough or a sink which can be filled with ericaceous mixture and then the plant will thrive and increase, spreading stems from the main rosette and from this mat of dark green pointed leaves come the beautiful blue trumpets some 2 in long with deeper blue and greenish-yellow markings on the outside. There is a pale blue and a white form, but the deep blue is, I think, the finest. I recently visited a garden where in a specially prepared bed there was a magnificent display of these gentians growing under tall trees and the whole bed was most effectively surrounded by logs, the brown bark setting off the bright colour of the flowers.

When the winter jasmine *Jasminum nudiflorum* is thoroughly pruned in spring, after giving its flower all winter, there are sure to be a solid mass of new shoots starting to bloom the following November. And it is one of the first sights I look for to start the flowering of my winter garden. However, should they be slow in opening, they can be cut for the house and enjoyed

Figure 1.5: *Schizostylis coccinea*

Figure 1.6 *Jasminum nudiflorum*

at close quarters. Though with some scent, I do not think this jasmine compares with the intense perfume of the pink and white summer varieties. It is the flowering twigs *en masse* which make such a bright patch of colour on a winter's day, sometimes cascading from the wall of a house, or massed over a low parapet, or hard pruned into a hump of sprays in the rockery.

A tender shrub from Chile, *Eccremocarpus scaber*, is such an easy grower and will climb very quickly and cover or scramble through another plant. The pale green foliage has tendrils to entwine and hold it up as it moves. The cluster of orange tubular flowers produce large heads of seed, which will provide new plants for the following year, should the main one collapse from the cold. But if the base is well-covered with leaves or compost, even though the upper part may not survive, it will break from this base next summer and flower right through November until a heavy frost halts its progress. It is not really a true winter flowerer out of doors, but like so many other summer and autumn plants, if carefully sited it can be counted on for November blooms, before it succumbs to the cold.

Another wall lover with very showy flowers, but of three colours, is *Abutilon megapotamicum* or *vexillarium*. This will flower into November too, before being cut by frost, in the same way as the eccremocarpus. The blooms hang down like a red bell with yellow petals issuing from below and purple-brown anthers showing within. These colourful flowers cluster along the stem below the vine-shaped serrated leaves, making a very striking shrub. My father had a large plant of this covering a southern, but quite exposed, wall of his house; and mine is growing in a right-angled corner, warm and safe, I hope, from cold sea gales. When the flowering has finally ceased the shrub can be pruned and shaped so that any protection it may need later on is easier to manage. There is a variegated form of this plant which I think is quite horrible, the leaves being mottled, with sickly yellow blotches. They quite ruin the effect of the blooms, muddling up their colour with the bright yellow part of the flower. But I have yet to come across a variegated form of any plant that I found more desirable than the common type. But, luckily, it is each to his own taste ... in the garden.

Some of the osmanthus group of shrubs are very attractive plants to have growing, most of them flowering during the winter period. As their name, from the Greek, means scented flower, they all are, certainly, very sweetly perfumed. From September onwards, the Japanese variety O. *aquifolium*, or *ilicifolius* but now known as *heterophyllus*, starts to bloom — it is really quite tricky keeping up with all the name changes, especially when one has had the plant a long time! My osmanthus is about twenty years old and around 8 ft sq, growing in some sun but under the partial shade of big apple trees. I planted it so that the fragrant bunches of creamy-white flowers, which appear tucked in at the base of the leaves, would give a pleasant lemon scent to the air in a spot at the top of the lawn where we sit

31

and have tea towards the tail end of summer. At a casual glance it looks like a holly bush, but in fact the leaves grow opposite each other, whereas the holly leaves grow alternately. Though the leaves were prickly when my plant was young, they are now smooth and more like the spring-flowering *O. delavayi* from China.

There are two kinds of snowdrop which flower through November, *Galanthus nivalis reginae-olgae* (named after Queen Olga of Greece) and then *G. corcyrensis*, the first appearing before its leaves and the second flowering among its leaves. They are only a couple of the fifty species or distinct cultivars of snowdrop offered by one of the specialist bulb nurseries, and the flowering period covers September to April, with the peak time around February. The different kinds are worth acquiring as they vary in height and leaf form, some flowers being pure white and some tipped or based with green. A rare snowdrop named G. 'Lady Elphinstone' is yellow, and rather expensive. But one bulb could be cosseted and enjoyed for its scarcity, though it's a risk as it can revert! But I think gardening must be exciting, to be rewarding.

After the autumn-flowering crocus have finished there are three varieties I like, all about 4 in high, that grace us with their appearance in November. *C. salzmannii* is a soft lilac from Morocco, blooming among a cluster of green leaves; then comes *C. medius*, a great favourite from the South of France which grows very freely and has dramatic colouring of dark purple-veined flowers, with bright red stamens. Last is *C. longiflorus*, a light violet, which appears after the leaves and shows vermilion stigmata. These all thrive in neutral soil in a sunny spot in the rockery or in drifts on a grassy bank; and the subtle differences in their colourings are a great asset to the winter flowers during this month.

There are one or two plants such as the *Coronilla glauca* and *Acacia longifolia* that flower virtually all the year round, given a situation in sun and shelter; and a curiously flowered little shrub that does this and is one of my favourites is *Grevillea alpina*. It never reaches more than a foot high so it looks very good among the winter-flowering heathers in the rockery, tucked against the protection a rockside gives. The foliage is a little like a rosemary and the unusual spidery flowers hang in a cluster of red wands from cream blobs touched with green. It likes a light, acid, peaty soil and will then settle down and remain in bloom from January to December, so it cannot be pigeon-holed into any particular month for flower. I include it in November, as there it is, with its red and glossy green colouring, at the beginning of the winter months — one of the prettiest little plants to have in the garden and well worth protecting which is easy to do as it is so small. It comes from south Australia so to mitigate the disappointment of a loss in very severe winters, cuttings can be taken in July and over-wintered in pots.

To complement the little *Cyclamen coum* flowering during the first few months of the year and towards the end of winter, *C. neapolitanum* (now called the far less evocative name *hederifolium*) is in bloom as winter starts, pushing up its tiny rich pink flowers through the thicket of falling autumn leaves, sometimes before its own leaves appear. *C. neapolitanum album* has slightly larger flowers and of a pure white, unlike the *C. coum album* which is very rarely totally white, but has crimson staining at the base which is nevertheless very attractive. All these cyclamen take a little time to get established but eventually make a carpet of colour right through the winter and will grow even under beech trees, provided the drainage is good. In my garden, and in a beautiful garden which my sister once had where I was given my original cyclamen, they grow on sloping ground under a light canopy of trees. Some of my plants I have grown from seed, but great patience was needed to wait for those results!

Most of the colchicums usually flower too early to be included in the winter garden. Often wrongly called autumn crocus, they are of the lily family and I find that they thrive better in short grass because the flowers appear on their own and need some support, should there be any breeze. The leaves are large and take up a good deal of room and in some ways, therefore, these bulbs are best planted in a place in the herbaceous border where the conspicuous foliage will not be out of place when it comes after the flowers, as it is inclined to look so in turf unless this is kept fairly rough. The lovely globular cups are various shades of mauve through pink to lilac and there is a superb white, *C. speciosum album*. A variety from the Greek islands that does flower right through November is *C. variegatum* with deep-rose goblets. Colchicums can look rather surprising, standing — with any luck — upright with their bare white stems, which accounts for their nick-name of naked ladies or naked boys. So they do need careful siting to give their best effect and will not thrive in shade. The pink-flowered *C. lusitanicum* from Portugal is another choice November bloom.

Long ago a friend gave me a small clump of a dwarf michaelmas daisy, a hybrid belonging to the *Aster* family. Every year in late autumn it becomes a mat 4 in high of lavender-pink blooms with yellow button centres. It lasts for weeks in flower and requires no attention, bar the removal of the dead stems in the spring. It is so nice and stubby that it needs no staking, although it is in the path of the prevailing westerly wind. Growing beside a bay tree in front of the potting shed, it has a very sunny position but doesn't seem to dry out. I wish all my plants gave so little trouble.

In these last two weeks of the month my winter flowers have got well into their stride and I note with great pleasure all the buds ready to open, either tucked away on the evergreen bushes or suddenly exposed to view as the autumn leaves of the deciduous plants fall away and leave their host to fight out the cold alone. Rather cowardly in a way as they choose not to appear again till life is easy once more and somehow the bad days have been defeated. Occasionally, of course, the weather triumphs and a bush, with or without leaf protection, dies; with foresight, cuttings of that particular plant have been judiciously struck, so that the progeny can live.

Chapter 2

December

As December begins it is really wintertime, but although the days are so short there can be quite a range of temperatures, sometimes dull or sunny, mild or frosty; so I am prepared for anything, but I don't usually find I have to bring out all my protection guns until after Christmas. When the climate is variable, and warm wet weather can make the plants soft and sap-laden, they are not hardened up for a cold spell and the tenderised stems of the delicate species will burst, if not watched later and wrapped with felt. Conversely a cool dry spell — but not windy-dry, which is the most damaging of all — will toughen up and prepare the tender plants so that they withstand quite nasty bouts of frost and snow very well. But for prolonged and heavy cold it is necessary to be ready with emergency treatment. A walk round the garden to keep an eye on things will warn of wind damage with root-rocked holes which will soon let in water and cold and set up disease, or a check to note what size of box will be needed by a plant which may have grown since last winter and want a bigger cover than before. Then when and if the bad weather comes, everything is to hand. I must admit I am rarely in this position, but I plan how I should be!

From the honeysuckle family come two bush species from China which start to flower in early December and last till the end of winter. Like so many of the plants of this time of year their creamy flowers are highly scented, and this benefit can be used to the very best effect if the shrubs are planted near the house and particularly not far from doors or windows. The blooms come at the axil where the leaves join the slightly reddish stem in pairs. In a mild winter, the leaves hang on and hide the flowers, but by the turn of the year, if not before, the bush will be bare of leaf; and, if properly pruned and even, I find, sheared two or three times during the year to keep a nice round shape, all through the coldest months the shrub will be clouded with delicate pale blooms. *Lonicera fragrantissima* has the most intensely scented flowers but they are very slightly smaller than *L.*

Figure 2.1: *Lonicera fragrantissima*

Figure 2.2:
Camellia sasanqua

standishii. Fortunately there is a cross between these two, *L. × purpusii*, which seems to have the blessings of both parents and the variety 'Winter Beauty' has branches massed with flowers, which last for many weeks; and none of the blooms is affected by frost. So I think these bushes are real winter treasures, easy to grow in any soil, and a delight to see and to smell on a dark cold day.

Many people are familiar with the summer-flowering deciduous buddleias which grow so quickly after their harsh pruning in February, and whose blossoms are such a draw for the butterflies. There are several winter varieties which are evergreen and from more tropical climates, but very worth while siting carefully for maximum protection. I have grown *B. auriculata* (from South Africa) under a south window and the 2 in sprays of white flowers, with a touch of yellow eye, are wonderfully honey-scented. The leaves have white felted undersides like those of the gazania plant. This buddleia is pruned in the spring and strikes easily from cuttings. I am looking now for a really protected place in my garden to try and grow either *B. officinalis* with its pale mauve 6 in flowers, or *B. asiatica* which has lemon-scented drooping white sprays. But there is a hybrid between *B. asiatica* and one with beautiful canary-yellow flower spikes from Madagascar, *B. madagascariensis*, which has been named *B. × lewisiana* 'Margaret Pike' and this has butter-yellow sprays and I think would look really stunning, and be protected, against a white wall of the house. But I understand the cold here will often cause it to lose its leaves, though this did not befall my *B. auriculata*, so I think it's well worth a try.

My favourite camellias are the *sasanqua* species, for their flowers are scented unlike the majority of the main range of spring-flowering camellias. The leaves are smaller and neater and so are the flowers, but as they bloom early in December, well before the larger-flowered *C. japonica* and *C. × williamsii* varieties, they have no competition and stand on their own, giving colour and perfume amongst their shiny leaves. For some years I grew the white *C. sasanqua* 'Narumi-gata' in a fairly exposed position by the front gate. I remember it was in flower one year in early December, for I picked and wore the blossoms at my daughter's wedding. The scent still brings back that episode. Unfortunately, I planted a mimosa *Acacia longifolia* nearby and this grew so large and towered above the poor camellia. So I don't really know whether it succumbed because of the exposed position or because of the impoverishment of the soil as the mimosa grew like wildfire.

I replaced it with another plant and also bought a red one, *C. sasanqua* 'Crimson King'; and for a year or two kept them in pots in the garden most of the year, but carried them into the greenhouse when the gales blew. Their flowers, of course, with the added warmth, were twice the normal size, but the shrubs became too large to carry and some years ago I planted them in a sheltered bed where frost, I hope, passes them by, and the wind is not too fierce. They have settled down and grown well and flowered successfully too. My only regret is that they are not near the house, so I have to go down the garden and see them in flower and catch their scent, which is fine on a pleasant day but not worth venturing so far on a bad one. I have had to plant my shrubs in a good ericaceous mixture and dress with peat and leaf-mould as my clay soil is not really suitable for camellias, though they can tolerate it better than rhododendrons. But at least the bed where they are planted is in full sun most of the year. For these winter species flower so early that they need more sun than the ordinary camellias to help ripen the wood and set the flowers.

Around the garden I have different sizes of the shrub — and in one case a 20 ft tree — of *Viburnum tinus*, known as 'Laurustinus'. During the winter these will stay in flower continuously, the dark evergreen leaves showing up the pure white flowers from pinkish buds. Though this plant comes from the Mediterranean regions, it is remarkably hardy and will put up with any fury in the weather. The large tree in full sun comes into flower at the end of October, but a small shrub which I have to keep pruned as it abuts on to a path, produces its flowers gradually. I have cut these trees to the ground when they get too leggy and then they can be kept a nice neat shape with pruning, but they do not produce any flowers for the first winter after the initial ground-prune. Where there is room to let them have their head it is a fine sight to have the backdrop all winter of the massed white flowers covering the height of the whole tree. The flower scent of this viburnum is not nearly as good as V. × *bodnantense* but it gives a totally different appearance, making a solid block of leaf and flower, whereas the scented tree is twiggy and spare without its leaves, giving a very delicate lacy effect. Both are first class and form the basis of the winter-flowering garden, as they are never without bloom from November to March.

I always know when the summer is over because the spikes of bloom on the pampas grass, *Cortaderia selloana*, from Argentina, suddenly make their appearance out of their circular mass of razor-sharp knife-thin leaves. When they unfurl, for a few days their creamy fronds are quite breath-taking against a blue sky or mirrored in water; but coming at a time when the season is turning over, so often a strong gale or heavy rainstorm will blow them sideways or clot the delicate feathery sprays into a mush. Nevertheless, in a more protected place and even as mine is — standing in the middle of the lawn facing the westerly gales — most of the plumes remain for many weeks till well after Christmas, making a great feature in the garden. In February or March, as the leaves become brown and dry, I shear my plant hard back round the edge and in the centre, for the plant forms a ring like a doughnut. One year I sprinkled Growmore in the middle to give it a boost, but it always produces about two dozen blooms, as it was planted correctly, long before I came to the garden, in full sun on a well-drained slope of the lawn. Some experts recommend burning the foliage in the spring, instead of shearing, to clean out all the dried debris, but I can't face doing this because I'm sure masses of little animals make it their home and certainly my cats use the cascading leaves to shelter from the rain or cool themselves on a sunny day; and, I fear, in order to catch some of the inhabitants!

The mimosa, *Acacia longifolia*, which grew to 20 ft at the front gate, and I believe damaged with its non-compostable leaves the camellia growing beneath it, became a great talking-point of the garden, flowering on and off all the year and right through the winter before succumbing and suddenly dying on me one September after a very long period of drought. Quite unexpected with this particular shrub which grows so freely in sunnier drier climes. I brought back a tiny plant about 6 in high the next time I visited Provence in the South of France, to replace my lost one. I found it among one of thousands of seedlings growing on the side of a mountain above the sea. This time I planted it in the best place I had in a south corner of the house and after taking a year or two to put down roots it was suddenly above the window and weighed down with branches and sprays of fluffy balls of yellow flower. Unfortunately we had a freak northerly gale which caught the top-heavy tree and brought it down. Patching was done and stakes applied, too late, but the main stem was practically severed. I realised it could not be saved and sawed it in a clean break, tying in three or four little branches which remained and which I hope and expect will grow up and take over. But I lost hundreds of flowers and it was some weeks before a few blooms appeared again. This was a lesson to me in not watching and staking in time, or ideally, when planting. But the mimosa had been pencil-thin when I put it in and it caught me unawares! The flowers are very similar to the feathery February-flowering *A. dealbata* but the leaves are long and slim and it is a little hardier. Luckily both are deliciously scented. Although it is evergreen, when it discards its old leaves they remain very hard and inflexible and do not break down well for compost. But this is a small drawback for such a continuous flowerer.

In another bed on the south wall I have a *Gazania splendens* hugging the warm bricks and it has survived for years, the bright orange flowers with black centres opening whenever the sun shines, even in the depths of winter. In a very severe spell of frost I have placed a cardboard box over the roots to stop the white-felted leaves and stems being frozen as their fluffy thickness makes them much more susceptible to freezing than a hard dry leaf or stem. It is necessary to guard against the cold rupturing the fleshy leaves which, as the water in them freezes, burst; something to watch for when growing plants from a part of the world where they naturally stand up to great heat and drought by storing fluid within their leaves.

There are so many shades of helleborus, and various forms of growth, some making little herbaceous rockery plants and others being shrubby and becoming 3 ft evergreen bushes. From now on different colours will carry on right through the winter. The best known kind is the Christmas Rose, *H. niger*, so perfect when grown correctly, but so often a muddy mess of slug-chewed grey! Some gardeners suggest a cloche over the plant so that the flowers rise clean out of the ground beside their leaves and avoid the spattering from the rain. An easier way, I think, is to put leaf-mould or compost right round the plant in autumn, for they like rich feeding in any case, as long as the soil is well-drained. Then the little mound above the soil gives the flowers a chance to keep clean. Another idea with these low-growing hellebores is to cover the surrounding surface with moss to prevent the mud from splashing the blooms.

These plants are a member of the buttercup family and their flowers are like large buttercups — they can be up to 5 in across — and the colours range from white to green and pink to darkest maroon. Yellow is uncommon, though among the *H. orientalis* group, which flowers from February to April (the so-called Lenten Rose) there is a rare yellow *H. kochii* and a newer one called 'Ingot'.

But after the *H. niger* with its white flowers and various larger forms, some tinted with pink on the reverse, the first purple one appears, usually by the end of December. I have grown this dramatic *H. atrorubens* in the rockery and the fine aubergine-dark blooms are a favourite colour of mine and very showy as they stand straight up, well clear of the coming foliage and a good 12 in high. *H. nigricors* is also tall-growing and a hybrid of *H. niger* and *H. lividus corsicus* — a later-flowering Corsican hellebore — and will start to flower before Christmas with creamy-green blooms on reddish stems. These also stand up well above the elegant leaves as do the flowers of *H. atrorubens*. The leaves of the various kinds differ greatly in shape and style, some, like *H. corsicus*, having serrated edges. Most of the varieties like the sun, especially when they come from the Mediterranean region, though *H. orientalis*, the Lenten Rose seems, with *H. niger*, to prefer the shadier part of the garden. And *H. foetidus*, in my garden, thrives under trees in a good deal of shade and I believe will tolerate complete lack of sun.

There are a number of heathers that flower in winter; in fact it is possible to find a plant for every month of the year. The *Erica carnea* varieties grow well in my clay soil, though I plant them in pockets of the rockery and break up the ground with peat. One plant which begins to flower in December is *E. carnea* 'Winter Beauty', very like *E. carnea* 'King George' which, with me, is in flower in February — but with slightly deeper pink little blooms. And another lime-tolerant heather is *Erica darleyensis* also known as 'Darley Dale'. This plant will flower for many weeks and the pale pink shoots, growing slightly taller than the *carnea* group, will make a good ground cover with their dense growth.

Forming a continuous display till the end of the year the *Schizostylis* 'Mrs Hegarty' and *S.* 'Viscountess Byng' flower during December after the lovely red *S. coccinea*, which first opens its blooms at the end of the summer, has given way to the S. 'November Pink'. Their salmon and rose-pink flower stalks last a number of weeks and the clumps of fine sword-like leaves will increase over the years to cover a large area of the bed, so if a corner can be found that is not too prominent in the garden — but one that gets a good baking of summer sun but where the soil is not too dry — then there is a wonderful dividend of these attractive sprays of flowers when the days are at their shortest and often gloomiest.

Some of the strangest looking flowers in the winter garden are the chrome-yellow curly puffs clinging like a spider to the bare branches of the Witch Hazel or *Hamamelis mollis* and giving off a sweet aromatic scent. Of the various types, the first one to flower does so as early as November, the lemon petals unfortunately hidden by the leaves, but this form, *H. virginiana*, produces an oil which is distilled from the bark and used as a remedy for bruising, and to staunch bleeding. But in flower by December, the commonest hamamelis and I think the best, because it has the largest flowers, is the Chinese species, *H. mollis*, found in the Yangtze valley and introduced in the West in 1879. This does not grow to a great size, reaching eventually 8-9 ft, the Japanese kind *H. japonica* var. *arborea* being a better choice when there is room to grow it against a north wall, where it will reach 25 ft, its fan-shaped branches covered with tawny-yellow blooms touched with claret at the base. Background is important with these delicate blooms; they will obviously show up much better on a white wall as they tend to blend into and get lost against a red-brick one.

There are two attractive variations in flower colour I like with the *H. mollis*. One, *H. mollis* 'Pallida' with very pale yellow blooms, long-petalled; and the other *H. mollis* 'Brevipetala' where the stubby clusters are a warm orange. And there are around a dozen hybrids between *H. mollis* and *H. japonica*, one *H. × intermedia* 'Carmine Red' has large round leaves and very large red flowers too. All the witch hazels have different shaped leaves, some of which turn colour before they fall, but this is not a feature that appeals to me personally. Two other good flower shades are *H. × intermedia* 'Ruby Glow' a rich copper, and *H. × intermedia* 'Jelena' a bronzy-orange mass of curls. But with all of these — and there are many others — it takes a lot to beat the scent of *H. mollis*.

Hamamelis like a deep rich soil but will not tolerate too much lime. The best way to prune is to cut awkward branches for the house, to keep a nice shape, for very little trimming is needed otherwise.

In a narrow raised bed at the top of my terrace, which is sun-baked in summer but gets no direct sun in winter, a group of the Grecian *Crocus laevigatus* push up their pale lilac flowers every year, after their summer cooking, and display their spherical cups, finely marked on the outside, as if by an artist's hand, with deeper lilac stripes. There is a form *C. laevigatus fortenayi* which has slightly larger flowers. Then from nearby southern Italy comes *C. imperati* which has a beige background to the prominent stripes, so they look very different when closed. But the sun opens them to show a

Figure 2.3: *Hamamelis mollis*

clear mauve lining, and at the base a chrome yellow throat. These two complementing crocus species are a very pleasant sight, even when the French windows are shut against the cold and they have to be viewed through the glass, but infinitely lovelier seen close to, when the weather allows a walk outdoors around Christmas time. A true herald of the spring.

Another osmanthus which follows the blooming of O. heterophyllus in November, and begins to flower any time from now on until March is O. suavis. It has shiny dark green, spear-like leaves with little tooths along the edges. The clusters of flowers, though small, are very sweetly scented like all osmanthus, and the bushes rarely grow to reach more than 5 ft sq and are happy in any good soil. Grown in a bed, surrounded by other shrubs to give some protection and a little shade, this Himalayan plant is, I believe, a very choice winter acquisition to have in the garden.

Two little cyclamen for this month are C. hiemale and C. ibericum. They look very like C. coum which starts to flower in January and in fact these are often now grouped under coum but they are a little taller, about 4 in and the leaves, though round and shiny and a dark green, have white marblings round the middle of the leaf. The flowers are a slightly different shade of magenta and the darker staining at the base in C. hiemale is round, and in C. ibericum is triangular. These very slight differences must have been very exciting for those lucky enough to look for, and find them, in their native habitat. But any of them are treasures, and make a field of colour in time in a good leafy soil, and look at their best naturalised under the protective half-shade of trees, or in the warmth reflected from the stones of a snug place in the rockery. For the corms, in whatever situation they are in, do seem to like to be dry — they will not put up with sogginess.

I don't know of any texture in a flower to match the shiny velvet plush of a pansy, Viola tricolour 'Winter Flowering', and the seed can be sown in early summer and then the flowers will appear at the beginning of winter, and if the little plants are regularly dead-headed they will go on producing their blooms through the chilly months, showing their white, violet, yellow and garnet-red faces like cheerful kittens. There is a Viola rothamagensis (from Rouen in France) that flowers practically the year round giving a profusion of small mauve pansies from a neat clump of grass-green leaves, but I haven't yet managed to track this down for my garden.

The little violas are of the same species, but have smaller flowers on more compact plants; and two I find enchanting are V. florariensis, a blue and white tufted viola about 6 in high, a natural hybrid from Geneva, and V. gracilis a tiny purple one from Greece with a yellow eye.

There are so many species and varieties of snowdrop, in fact a nursery lists over sixty, but one of the prettiest and earliest, which flowers any time from November to January, but is at its best in December with me, is the 4 in high Galanthus byzantinus from eastern Europe. It likes to be in a neutral soil and will form a patch 3 in sq of its large white and green bells.

This variety prefers warmer and sunnier places — because of the area it comes from — than the common G. *nivalis*, which is quite happy in any situation, even woodland moisture. And the leaves of G. *byzantinus* are not a bright green as in many snowdrops, but a rather attractive grey colour. All the snowdrops are best divided for re-planting just as the flowers are going over, so that you can see what you are doing. If starting with new bulbs, work quickly for they are very small and dry rapidly, with unsatisfactory results, that is . . . they do not come up!

By now *Chimonanthus praecox*, the Winter Sweet, will be opening its translucent yellow flowers with their curious wax-like texture and maroon inner petals. And this is one of the strongest scents of the winter flowerers and although rather a slow-growing shrub and loath to flower in its first few years, especially if in rich soil, once established it seems impervious to any kind of bad weather and I think it is well worth waiting for in the garden. It can be helped to flower a little earlier when grown against a wall, because, of course, the summer sun, which ripens the wood, will be more potent when reflected back, particularly from bricks rather than a wooden fence. Cuttings are difficult to strike and the best way to increase this choice plant is to peg down and make layered rootings in May of any lower limbs. And small plants which have been grown on for a few years make lovely presents, and the lucky recipients won't have to wait long for their first flowers, if you have done the donkey-work for them! There are two other forms of winter sweet, one with larger flowers, but it is not so scented, and another with lemon-yellow blooms with no darker marking, and again not so scented as C. *praecox*, which will go on producing flowers on its bare branches through to early March.

In a mild winter the old rhododendron, first hybridised in 1829, R. *nobleanum* 'Venustum', will flower for Christmas. It will grow slowly, to 10 ft eventually, and likes to be planted in an acid soil in a light woodland setting. The striking flowers are a rich pink with darker markings inside the cluster of funnels. The leaves are not shiny like some rhododendrons but a dull deep green with rusty undersides, for the cross was made between R. *arboreum* and R. *caucasicum*, the first a 40 ft tree-like species from the Himalayas and the second a 2 ft high very hardy plant from the Caucasus in South-West Asia, both of which have felty reverses to their leaves. There are varieties with plain white or unstained pink flowers, but I think the original cross is the most attractive one to plant. The blooms continue to appear, on and off, until March.

As the year dies there are often, in a mild season, still some of the plants which may have started their flowering in the summer, throwing out the occasional bloom to let us know their season is not dead as yet. There are the roses and chrysanthemums, if the frost has been gentle, and the bright yellow flowers of the hypericums and my ubiquitous brooms. I have a hedge of two or three plants of *Lavatera olbia* 'Rosea' which are in a very sunny border, but towering above them and making a protective canopy is

Figure 2.4: Winter Sweet — *Chimonanthus praecox*

an enormous fir tree, so the pink mallow flowers go on appearing much later than to be expected. My amazing gazania plant continues throughout the year unabated, as long as the spent blooms are removed, and a striking sub-shrub called the Californian Fuchsia, *Zauschneria californica*, if carefully planted in a hot sunny place in the rockery, can survive very low temperatures once established and will produce its bright scarlet tubular flowers above the narrow, ash-grey foliage, quite far into winter — as so many of the ordinary fuchsias do, until the daylight is too short for them and frost spoils the flowers and necessitates a peat or bracken covering to save their roots for next year.

But of the fifteen varieties of cistus which cheer my summer garden, one particularly, *C.* × *pulverulentus* 'Sunset', has a very long flowering period and puts out its cerise blooms, certainly until the end of December; and very often the odd flower will appear at any time during winter, its bright petals glowing among the aromatic and evergreen crinkly leaves massing the bush. *C. albidus* will also open the odd flower in winter, of a softer mauve with a fat boss of yellow stamens. The name refers to the whitish down on the undersides of the leaves.

So with careful positioning of the plants I see no reason why December should be drab in the garden. By putting the right shrub in the right place it will be encouraged to keep going, with no detrimental effects, until severe weather forces it to die down and then it can be helped by protecting its base, so that it will come through the hard times, ready to throw up shoots and begin its flowering season again in due course. But it is surprising how many plants will continue or come into flower under quite severe conditions, giving reward to the adventurous. And to see their flowers blooming under such adverse conditions, surely makes the extra thought and trouble necessary well worth it, for the pleasure the flowers give in return in lightening our spirits, which helps us through the winter.

Chapter 3

January

However mild the early winter has been, by the beginning of January colder weather with snow or frost can be expected and then I find the best way to look after the flowering plants and anticipate the protection and care they may need is to walk around the garden, if possible every day at some time — if only for a few minutes — and check how the plants are faring. A gale will have rocked and flattened some of the bushes and they will need re-staking and the hole near the stem filled in or water will rot it or disease destroy it. When there is a bad gale I find it is better to leave a bush that has bent down with the wind until all sign of the storm has abated and not try to set it up straight again where further battering will damage it even more, sometimes tearing off limbs and leaves. Possibly several days later, when you have waited patiently through the eye of the storm and put up with the returning half of the gale, then is the moment to prop up the poor plant and assess the size of cardboard box or other form of protection that may be needed in the next few weeks, should snow and ice set in, and attempt to freeze the bush into extermination.

The translucent glow of the *Coronilla glauca*, which comes from the bloom on the sea-green leaves as much as the acid-yellow flowers, is one of the brightest flowers with which to open the new year, though it actually gives its blooms right through the winter months and for many more. As it comes from southern Europe the plant appreciates some shelter; but although I grow my bush near the wall of the house, it is not protected from the prevailing westerly or occasional southerly gales, and has survived for many years now. The leaves are pinnate and closely mass the bush, making a fine setting for the bunches of bright pea flowers. It renews itself constantly and doesn't seem to need dead-heading, as so many other plants do, to ensure a succession of flowers.

Another luminous yellow bloom with an even stronger scent than the coronilla flower is the best-known feathery-leaved mimosa, *Acacia dealbata* known as the Silver Wattle, the name for mimosa in its native Australia. In warm areas it grows as an enormous free-standing tree, but in less favourable parts of the country it will thrive remarkably well with wall protection and grow 20-50 ft up to a roof and produce its sprays of fluffy yellow blooms in the first weeks of the year. These will last longer in the garden than indoors, for when brought into a room the little woolly balls of the flower desiccate and quickly lose their enchanting scent. I grow also *A. longifolia*, the Sydney Golden Wattle, which is the hardiest of the species and more tolerant of any lime in the soil.

The Ozark witch hazel, *Hamamelis vernalis* from Missouri, the American mid-West, follows on the other witch hazels which began flowering in December. With their curiously pungent scent, not as alluring as that of *H. mollis*, the flowers are clustered thickly on the branches and copper-coloured. The variety 'Sandra' has whitish-yellow blooms and is admired for its vividly changing leaf colour; so it is not on my short list. But for anyone who wants to plant for leaf shape, size, texture and colour, the hamamelis offer great variety.

A very unusual looking shrub or small tree which it has taken me a long time to grow fond of, as I failed to appreciate that the green catkins were flowers and it all looked too much of one colour for my taste, is the American plant garrya. It was so-named by the plant collector Douglas after a friend in the Hudson Bay Company who gave him great help in his north-west American expeditions. The most well-known variety is *G. elliptica*, with leaves like the evergreen oak and in the male plant, particularly, 6 in long catkins of silvery green flowers in January and February, which are very resistant to damage by frost. It enjoys having a wall behind it and thrives in coastal districts where it will reach 12 ft sq. It is not fussy as to type of soil as long as it is well-drained. During May the bushes should be trimmed to shape against the wall or to a rounded form, for the flowers come on the mature shoots of the previous year. Now I find the overlapping trusses of matt-green inflorescences rather intriguing with their velvety texture, but it is a very strange-looking plant.

There are many other prunus trees as well as the *P. subhirtella* 'Autumnalis' which is my particular favourite because of its long flowering period. *P. davidiana*, the Chinese peach, was introduced by the Abbé David in 1865 and makes a small upright tree 12-20 ft high. Because its pink flowers, an inch wide, come in January they can be damaged by frosts. So when grown in colder areas it flowers later and suffers less. But planted in the corner site of a wall or house with a suitable background to show up the flowers clustering the leafless branches, I think it is such a pleasure to see so early in the year, that it is worth finding a warm protected corner for it. My father chose the site for my 30 ft high *P. subhirtella* 'Autumnalis' with special regard to the background for the wreaths of flowers, planting it in a sloping bed so that I can stand below and beneath it and the whole tree is silhouetted whenever there is a clear blue sky. I am sure I would not have had the forethought then to think of planting it with that prospect in mind.

Another prunus to flower this month is the winter-flowering form of *P. incisa* the Japanese Fuji Cherry, aptly named 'Praecox'. This makes a shrub rather than a tree and the pink buds open to pure white flowers. Another form 'February Pink' often shows its blush-pink flowers as early as January too.

Correa backhousiana is one of an interesting small group of evergreens native to Australia and Tasmania and therefore needing the warmth of the southern areas of our climates. In colder parts of the north they need greenhouse protection. The variety that flowers right through the winter is *C. pulchella*, the blooms being of palest shell-pink. *C. backhousiana* has hanging groups of yellowish-green bell-like flowers, and given the help of a warm wall will flower in January. There are two or three others with cream and red flowers, the leaves being usually of two colours of green, with grey or white undersides, and of various shapes from oval to narrow. I had never come across any of these plants till friends showed me one they grow successfully.

Another little known but attractive evergreen shrub, which comes from California, *Arctostaphylos manzanita*, will flower in the south also, as early as January, but it must have an acid soil as it is of the ericaceous family and close to the rhododendrons. But unlike the latter it prefers a very sunny site. It should be planted in April or October and needs a moist peaty soil with plenty of leaf-mould, and should not be allowed to dry out — rather like the proverbial palm tree — head in fire, feet in water. The thick oval leaves against the reddish branches show up the bunches of pitcher-like white or pink flowers, not unlike the flowers of the arbutus or lily-of-the-valley. There are various other species of this unusual evergreen, not all of them tender and some small and prostrate. Their Greek name reflects the fact that the berries of this plant were eaten by bears.

A very cheerful sight in the New Year are the bright yellow cups of the Winter Aconite, *Eranthis*. This little tuber will naturalise in the moist soil under deciduous trees and although a little slow to settle down will eventually spread into good clumps. The flowers are about 3 in high in the common form, *E. hyemalis*, with an Elizabethan ruff of green just beneath the flower, above the carpet of delicate green leaves. *E. cilicica*, from Turkey, has shorter flowers of a deeper yellow and a slightly bronzy tint to the foliage. A hybrid between these two has produced even brighter larger flowers, *E.* × *tubergeniana*, the best form of this being named 'Guinea Gold', but it flowers later than the others and the best effect, I have found, is to mix the two and so provide a longer succession of flower. There is a rare white species from Japan, *E. pinnatifida*, which needs special care, but well worth tracking down to make an intriguing match, growing beside a group of snowdrops.

For January is the time the common snowdrop begins to flower. With all

Figure 3.1: Winter Aconite —
Eranthis ✕ *tubergeniana*

the other varieties, larger, touched with green or double, I don't believe anything can match the little *Galanthus nivalis*. It nearly always comes into flower at the most inauspicious time of the year when in the month of January long warm spring days seem so far away and Christmas celebrations and family gatherings are over and there is only the cost left to count! Then to go out in the garden and see this tiny bulb pushing up through the soil and producing a bell-like flower does give a leap to the heart. My plants grow in the rockery and have gradually spread themselves; I have never got round to dividing and transplanting any of them, they have appeared, sometimes, in the shade of other plants; for *G. nivalis* is quite happy in woodland, too, and looks great interplanted with the winter aconite.

Before December begins I always have one or two plants of primrose flowering between the warm stones of my paths. They seem impervious to the only weed-killer I use in my garden. I do water a powder, non-toxic to animals, into my paths and terraces and on the gravel drive, otherwise the weeds defeat me. Fortunately, it is only necessary to use it every other year. But the *Primula vulgaris* takes no notice of this treatment and continues to proliferate and come into flower all through the winter. Though it is a plant so easily taken for granted, it is really very beautiful with its soft butter-yellow flowers and deeper centres and the leaves surrounding the bunch of flowers are pale green and crinkly. The delicate scent immediately conjures up the freshness of spring to come and the longer warmer days.

I have a circular rose-bed with the North American tulip tree, *Liriodendron tulipifera*, growing in the centre and when the huge leaves of this tree have floated down at the first frost and the roses have finally produced their last few flowers and also dropped their leaves, a little ring of *Crocus ancyrensis* push up through the soil around the tree and produce their round-cupped orange blooms — the outside touched with purple — as the new year begins, the rich bright globes transforming the area into a flowering bed once again, before it has had time to lose any colour.

Rhododendron mucronulatum is a deciduous shrub which is one of the first rhododendrons to flower, sometimes by the end of the year. It will grow to 4 or 5 ft making a more upright and larger bush than the R. 'Praecox', which doesn't come into flower till February. The blooms are a bright magenta and massed on the bare branches, the whole plant making a slender dome of colour. In a very mild winter it will not lose its leaves, but even in a severe one the shrub is quite hardy, and if the opened flowers are damaged by sudden frost, the unopened buds are not affected and will often delay their blooming and so be undamaged. If prolonged cold is anticipated, some form of shelter rigged up, will be time well spent in order to protect this lovely plant, originally from Manchuria, which can give such bright colour so early in the year.

Another little early flowerer is the bulb *Iris histrioides* 'Major'. It is a

Figure 3.2: *Primula vulgaris*

stubby plant with tough squat royal-blue flowers consisting of three
segments; down the centre of each one runs a gold marking, slightly
speckled. A native of Turkey, it likes a sunny site and well-drained rather
stony soil. A group of them makes a bright patch between rocks and being
only 4 in they stand up to any weather and also being so short their full
charm can be viewed from above to greater effect than the taller iris, such
as *I. bakeriana*, from nearby Iran. This is 10 in high but, nevertheless,
useful to plant as it again blooms in January with ultramarine flowers and a
purple blotch spotted with white. Its leaves show it is from the *I. reticulata*
section, being cylindrical and hollow and finally growing taller than the
flower.

A half-evergreen viburnum which makes a medium-sized spreading
bush is the slightly uncommon *V. foetens*. It is covered all winter with
fragrant white flowers, which, like many of the other varieties, are pink in

the bud. It grows most happily in a heavy soil which will not dry out, and will tolerate a northern aspect; and some overhead shade will protect the blooms from frost. It is closely allied to *V. × burkwoodii*, but I think has a slightly grander appearance with its large shiny leaves and thick smooth stems tipped with the cluster of felty flowers.

The Winter Heliotrope, *Petasites fragrans*, is a relative of the Coltsfoot and, literally, has rounded leaves in the shape of a colt's foot, large and green with white silky hairs underneath. In January or February it has the palest lilac daisy-type flowers of a wonderful heliotrope scent which are well worth picking, to perfume a room indoors. Though originally from the Mediterranean region, it is to be found naturalised in several neighbouring countries. If planted in a garden, it must be watched carefully or it will take over a whole area, so it is best grown in a wild part in light woodland where it can let itself go and discharge its wonderful scent into the winter air. It does appreciate some shelter as the fleshy stems are damaged by hard frost.

Most of the corylus, the Hazel Nut or Filbert trees, grow too large for the normal garden, but there is one kind, *C. avellana* 'Contorta', the Corkscrew Hazel, which develops very slowly to no more than 9 ft. From the Bonsai-like twisted branches primrose-yellow male flowers, borne on drooping catkins, hang in attractive groups during January and February, their very straightness such a marked contrast to the contorted branches they come from. The corylus thrive on chalk soils and prefer to be sheltered from cold winds.

All through January the *Chimonanthus praecox* or Winter Sweet, and once known as *Meratia praecox*, will be scenting the air with its pungent fragrance, however fierce the weather proves to be. Being so slow-growing it hardly ever needs pruning, but as the stems as well as the flowers are scented, a few pieces cut to shape the bush can be enjoyed away from the wind and rain and the smell is really good and strong when they are placed in the linen cupboard.

One of the earliest camellias of the *japonica* group to flower is a very lovely white one, *C. japonica* 'Nobilissima'. From a distance it can look very like a gardenia when in flower, a confusion I made for many years with a beautiful and enormous white bush I saw growing in an unreachable sunken garden, until I realised it must be a camellia as we cannot grow gardenias with any success out of doors in this country. The variety G. *thunbergia* does flower in winter and opens in the evening with exceptionally fragrant flowers, but must have glasshouse protection. But luckily, it was discovered that camellias are remarkably hardy. In Victorian times they were always grown in greenhouses and certainly under these conditions the flowers remain unspoiled and attain a great size; but gradually it was found that the bushes themselves are absolutely happy outside, particularly the *C. × williamsii* hybrids which will flower in even colder areas than the *C. japonica* types. A very tough plant with masses of white

Figure 3.3: *Iris histrioides* 'Major'

flowers set against bronze leaves is C. 'Cornish Snow' (*cuspidata* × *saluenensis*), but the white camellia I grow and which flowers this month is the C. *japonica* 'Nobilissima' which has double white flowers with a faint yellow tint. I have planted it with plenty of coarse peat in a bed where my clay soil is not too heavy and has been well incorporated with compost and leaf-mould over the years. Also, I am growing the camellia as one of a row to make a hedge, a way they are frequently grown abroad, but not so often here, where they are usually treated as individual specimens.

In Japan, where camellias grow so well, they are given more sun than we allow, as it is drier and there is no wet morning dew to damage the flowers. Nevertheless, I find they do not like to be in too shaded a woodland setting, like some rhododendrons. A nice ration of sun ripens the wood and sets the flowers for the following year. Near deciduous trees their flowers have some protection, yet the leaves and bark can get decent light.

Against a low wall at the bottom of my terrace is an old plant of *Chaenomeles* × *superba* 'Pink Lady'. It grows in very poor soil and gets no sun except in high summer when the arc of the sun's path reaches right round the garden and hits this wall for a few hours. This must be just enough to ripen the wood, for in January the spiky bare-branched shrub is coated with little cups of bright pink flowers. Lately it has grown to reach up to the top of the terrace wall and so can be seen from the house, but the main pleasure is when walking across the lawn this bright mass of colour on the sandstone wall gives an unexpected winter surprise. In the main herbaceous and shrub border at the bottom of the garden is a large 6 ft sq bush of C. *speciosa* 'Umbilicata' whose salmon buds are visible now, but will bloom properly during February. These chaenomeles are a marvellous group of shrubs to have in the garden as they will stand any treatment — soil or pruning or situation — and reward you with bright blooms totally impervious to frost, for many months of the year.

There are three other varieties in the C. *speciosa* group that I want to grow. 'Nivalis', a pure white with large flowers and 'Moerloosei' and 'Phylis Moore' the first being pink and white and the second almond pink. The seven different kinds I have at the moment are all strong pinks, or oranges or dark reds and I hanker suddenly for the delicate shades. So I am busy planning where I shall put them. When I first had my garden over thirty years ago I tended to buy first and think where to plant something afterwards. Now I am a little wiser, having lost many plants through having placed them in unsuitable sites. But it is a good way to learn, though a hard and, nowadays, an expensive way.

At the opposite end of the colour spectrum is the hellebore that flowers in this month, H. *colchicus*, from Colchis in Russia, whose blooms are the deepest maroon and the darkest of all this species. It likes to grow in a moist limy soil, even damper than usual for these plants, and the deep purple flowers of five petals glow like garnets against the shiny dark green leaves. A rather rare and choice plant to have in the garden. But once you

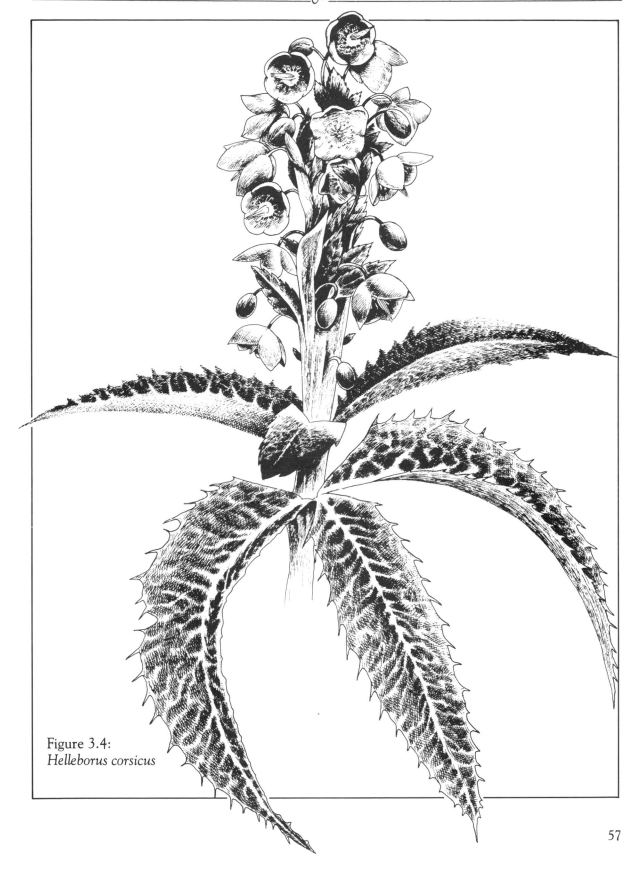

Figure 3.4:
Helleborus corsicus

have tracked down and bought one, this can be increased by division, to give more groupings, even though the main plant resents disturbance.

H. corsicus and *H. lividus* are two very similar evergreen shrubby plants, coming from an area of the Mediterranean very close to each other, Corsica and Majorca. They are not happy in dense shade like *H. foetidus*, which flowers earlier, but prefer some sun, if only from under deciduous trees, and a well-drained neutral soil. They have very handsome three-lobed glossy green leaves, marbled and veined with white, their edges frilled with spines. In March the cluster of apple-green flowers, with a slight yellow tinge, opens wide from and above the thick central 2 ft high stem.

There are two clematis I like very much that flower in winter; they are rather similar to each other, and I find often confused in books and catalogues. *C. cirrhosa* has finely-cut glossy leaves and creamy bell-shaped flowers, whereas another form of *C. cirrhosa*, also known as *C. calycina*, comes from the Balearic Islands; this *C. cirrhosa* (*calycina*) *balearica* has apple-green, more open flowers like a eucryphia, purple-spotted inside and the even-more delicately cut leaves turn bronze in the winter. *C. cirrhosa* doesn't begin to flower till January and continues for several weeks when the puffs of seed-heads develop. *C. cirrhosa* (*calycina*) *balearica* will put out the odd flower at any time during the winter from September to March. They are both a great asset to the winter garden, happy in most positions, even a north wall, as long as they have some sun and a well-drained soil.

There are several colchicums that flower in the early months of the year, but they are not as often seen as the rosy-lilac autumn-flowering *C. autumnale* and *C. speciosum*, and they have smaller flowers. But *C. luteum* is one I think is worth treasuring, as it is yellow unlike all the other varieties and from within the narrow leaves of the 3 in little plant long-stemmed golden flowers appear. Another neighbour of this pretty bulb, also from Afghanistan, *C. kesselringii*, is white with violet stripes. A pure white one to match the autumn white of *C. speciosum album*, but again smaller in size, is *C. brachyphyllum* from the Lebanon. These all like to be grown in sun in a neutral soil.

I find it is often worth going to the flower shows when I can, to see plants like these specialist bulbs in flower, and so make a personal choice. They will not be listed in the big catalogues, though there are, fortunately, a few growers who make a point of offering scarce and rare plants and bulbs.

Sometimes January can be mild, but occasionally the garden has to suffer the worst of weathers. But a very mild spell between two intensely cold periods, puts plants at extra risk and the violent differences in temperature strain their reserves to the utmost. And these unusual combinations cause havoc and can be universally applied. Luckily, heavy snow can often protect the plants from a freezing and drying wind. But I do believe the worst the plants have to suffer is, when after a spell of extreme mildness, the intense cold and cutting wind is followed by bitter weather again; each time the frost having much more effect on the moist sappy stems and leaves of the plants than if they had had a gradual cooling. Consequently they split open and the sap is lost, whereas a deep layer of snow would have saved them.

The tender plants do not recover, especially if they are of the broom and cistus family which will not break from the base again below the point where any shoots or leaf buds exist. Fortunately many plants, if covered up over their roots, though they are utterly destroyed above ground, will shoot miraculously in the spring from below the soil, as a herbaceous plant does. Those that have fleshy leaves, like mesembryanthemum, will stand ten degrees of frost for a few days, but if frozen too long they burst open and collapse and they do not break from the stem, even though this and the roots appear to be perfectly healthy and intact upon inspection next spring or summer.

So the important watchword for this time of the year is vigilance. The hardy trees and shrubs will come through a bad spell, even though they can temporarily look rather bedraggled. A few warmer sunny days will soon make them unfurl their tightly wrapped and protected buds again, those that were fully blooming when the frost struck will have often browned and fallen away, but three-quarters of the winter-flowering plants will survive most that can be thrown at them by our climate, and live to flower another day.

A boxed shelter, or even a piece of fine cloth, placed over a young and tender plant will halve the danger from cold and wind, and if a tree is well-grown and too big to cover, old carpet felt or hessian cut into strips and wrapped round and up the bark will preserve the sap rising in the stem, even though the foliage higher up may be frosted and damaged. As long as the bark does not split, new shoots will come from the stem next year and all is not lost. I treat my mimosa, *Acacia longifolia*, in this way as the trunk is now at least 2 in across. Then with care and a small amount of time and watchfulness, one of the worst months of the winter can be successfully handled.

Chapter 4

February

After nearly thirty years of gardening, I now find February the most exciting time of the garden year. It is the middle of winter and the days are still short and cold; and spring some way off. Now is the season when the careful planning and positioning of my winter-flowering plants will give their greatest reward. It is a period when some of the most scented flowers in the garden are in full bloom, for powerful scent is a speciality of so many flowers in winter.

I think my favourite plant which begins to bloom now is the *Daphne odora*, which grows into a nicely shaped bush with its glossy evergreen leaves. It bears waxy pink clusters of trumpet-shaped flowers, heavily and sweetly scented, so that my daphnes, which are strategically planted outside the back and front doors, are always seen and can be smelt as I go in or out. And they are near enough to catch the eye of a visitor, even on an inclement day, when suggestions to walk round the garden are greeted with little enthusiasm.

The variety of daphne with variegated leaves, *Daphne odora* 'Aureo-marginata', is hardier than the type. Fortunately the variegation consists of a pleasant narrow white edge to the polished green leaf, not the pallid effect some other variegated plants go in for.

This shrub is a native of China and Japan and will grow in any good soil and if given a sunny position by a wall to protect it from the worst weather it will, within a few years, become a well-shaped 4 ft sq bush. It requires no pruning and after the flush of its winter flowering over many weeks it makes a handsome glossy evergreen backdrop to the plants blooming around it during the rest of the year.

Two very attractive new hybrids are an evergreen *D. bholua* 'Gurkha' and a deciduous *D.* 'Jacqueline Postill', both of which have similar richly-scented pink flowers.

Another daphne which flowers in February is *D. mezereum*. I have never

Figure 4.1: *Daphne odora* 'Aureomarginata' outside the back door

been able to grow this variety. I have tried it many times, planting it in different parts of the garden, but it always dies. I finally gave up when an expert gardener told me it is temperamental and if it won't grow for you, you must acknowledge this; so I don't try any more. The bare branches are wreathed in waxy mauve buds; then the leaves come later with the very poisonous black berries. There is a white one, *D. mezereum* 'Alba' with ice-white flower clusters up the naked stems, followed by yellow, again poisonous, berries. I am not keen on dangerous plants in the garden, so I am now content to be without this variety, but can still admire it when I see it in other gardens; though I am sorry to be without its glorious scent.

The Spurge Laurel, *D. laureola*, is a native of Europe and has rather inconspicuous green flowers, but they are scented at night and as the plant will grow in shade and on heavy soil, it is well worth a place in a corner of the garden to add to the other flowers and scents of February. A dwarf variety, *D. laureola philippi*, from the Pyrenees is a good neat little bush for the rock garden.

I have recently lost a 20 ft high tree of *Stachyurus praecox*. It had taken many years to reach that height and is normally seen around 6-8 ft. I do miss my tree, for its sprays of yellow flowers hung on the leafless branches early in February and the elegantly pointed leaves which came later made a

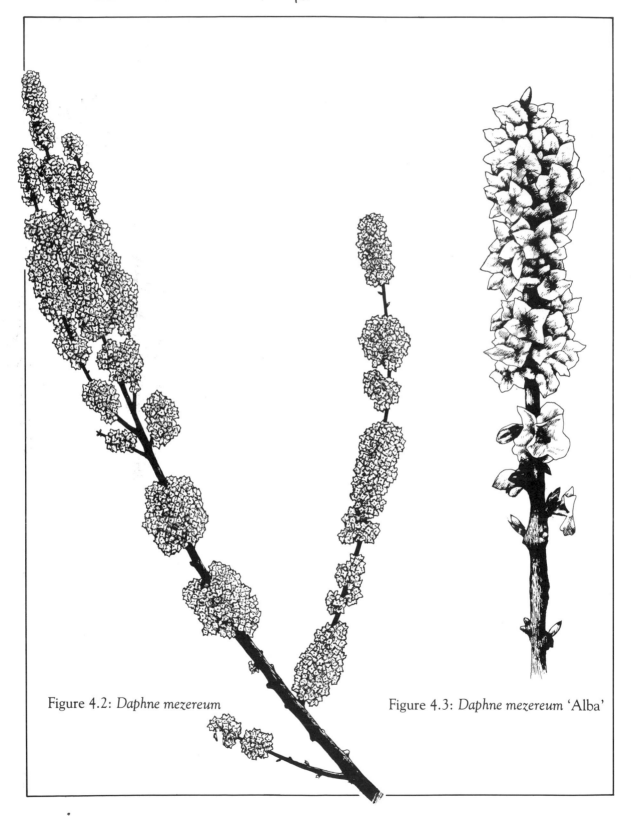

Figure 4.2: *Daphne mezereum*

Figure 4.3: *Daphne mezereum* 'Alba'

Figure 4.4: *Stachyurus praecox*

very striking foil the rest of the year, for they contrasted well with the small neat ones of the prunus tree growing beside it. I believe the dry summer of 1976 may have been the undoing of my stachyurus. I have a new one planted now and even more because it is a young plant I shall water it carefully and regularly, for it is not fussy as to soil. I prefer this variety from Japan as it flowers a few weeks earlier than *S. chinensis* from western China, which also has smaller, less impressive leaves.

Other natives of China and Japan and closely related to the witch hazels are the corylopsis plants. Their cowslip-scented clusters of flowers cover the branches and they will grow in sun or semi-shade, though the delicate pale-yellow blooms can be browned by a heavy frost. There are about eight or nine varieties, *C. pauciflora* being one of the earliest to flower with the smallest leaves, but these are pleasantly tinged with pink when young. I am growing this in a large pot as it is the one variety of the group that does not take kindly to my heavy clay soil. And I can also place the shrub against a wall for added protection in bad weather. But I have planted *C. spicata* in a protected place in the rockery, tucked in between an evergreen spring-flowering azalea and a summer-flowering cistus; so the yellow flowers should show up well and make a focal point, to be seen from the house windows on a winter's day.

A mahonia flowering in this month to end the winter, after the beautiful flowering of *M. lomariifolia* in November, is the variety *M. bealei*. My plant is old and, I am told, now quite rare, due to the confusion in nurseries over the last few years when *M. japonica* was offered as *M. bealei*, and gradually the true *M. bealei* is now disappearing. The plant has very large pinnate leaves and stiff sprays of strongly-scented yellow racemes thrown up from the centre of the stem, whereas the *M. japonica* sprays are finer and cascade like fronds. A very popular hybrid of *M. japonica* and *M. lomariifolia* is *M. × media* 'Charity', but it can be variable, and I prefer the three kinds I have, for their flower forms are distinctly individual. Curiously, the whole genus has yellow flowers, and yellow wood and young roots.

A pleasing shrub that flowers now and is, like the corylopsis, of the same family as the witch hazel (Hamamelis) which is already in bloom, is *Sycopsis sinensis*. But it has the great advantage of being evergreen with rich dark elliptical leaves and the flowers are rather unusual, having no petals, just yellow stamens tipped with crimson inside red-brown bracts. As it likes a shaded site, the sycopsis will do very well and grow to tree size on a north wall and it is a pleasure to turn a cold corner and see it flowering under such adverse conditions.

Another evergreen shade-lover is the Christmas Box, *Sarcococca*, which is happy in any soil, especially chalk. I have a plant of *S. humilis* still barely a foot high after several years, but it graces the rockery and the perfume from the clusters of white flower-sprays scent the cold winter air in February. I also have *S. hookeriana digyna* which is taller growing and has narrower leaves and smaller flowers, but in a bed near my back door it

1. *Iris unguicularis*

2. *Mahonia lomariifolia* against the house

3. *Rhododendron* 'Praecox'

4. *Myrtus communis tarentina*

5. *Viburnum tinus*

6. *Forsythia ovata*

7. *Crocus tomasinianus*

8. *Camellia japonica* 'Campbellii'

9. *Erica arborea* 'Alpina' in the rockery

10. *Rhododendron* 'Christmas Cheer'

11. *Magnolia stellata*

12. *Daphne odora* 'Aureomarginata'

16. *Clematis cirrhosa*

12. *Daphne odora* 'Aureomarginata'

13. *Mahonia bealei*

14. *Nerine bowdenii* under the bay window

15. *Helleborus orientalis* and *Eranthis hyemalis*

16. *Clematis cirrhosa*

17. *Cortaderia selloana*

18. *Coronilla glauca* near the front door

19. *Arbutus unedo*

20. *Schizostylis coccinea* 'Mrs Hegarty'

Figure 4.5: *Corylopsis pauciflora*

gives off quite a strong perfume. By the front door I have *S. confusa*, and all the bushes are well-shaped with their glossy leaves and twiggy bunches of flowers. I think they are a great asset to the winter flower list, especially as they can be squeezed into any shady corner of however small a garden.

Abeliophyllum distichum is not very well known, but a most useful shrub for this month. It has similiar flowers to the forsythia, but they are white and nicely scented and a branch crowded with blooms will last a long time if cut for the house. Though not seen in many gardens, this plant was introduced to Europe from Korea as long ago as 1924. It fares better when grown against a south wall, but is not particular as to soil. I find the bunched stems of starry-white flowers, touched with pink when in bud, do stand out and catch the eye on a dark day.

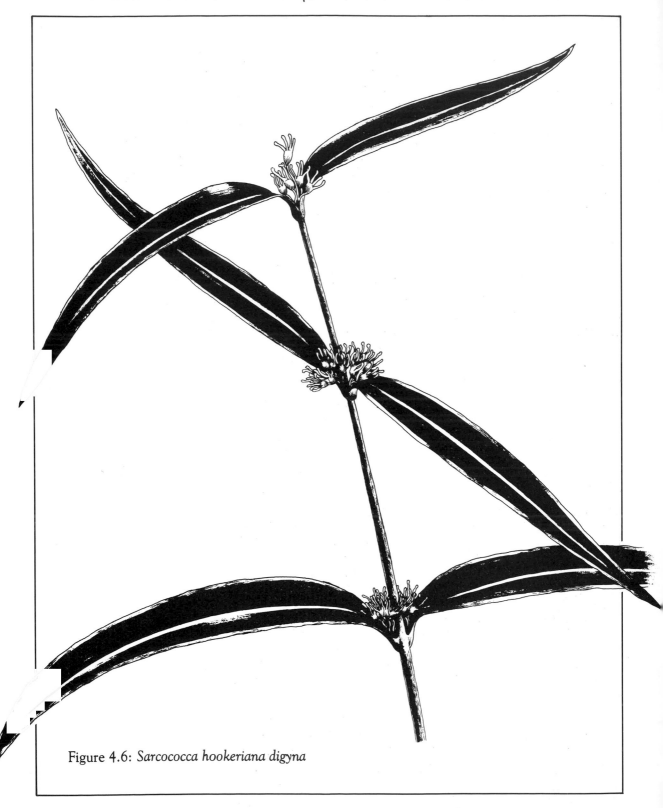

Figure 4.6: *Sarcococca hookeriana digyna*

Figure 4.7: *Abeliophyllum distichum*

When I look at my little tree of *Erica arborea* 'Alpina' it reminds me of the tree heaths I used to see growing in Provence in southern France, around the village of Cogolin, and which are used to make the best pipes for smoking. The foliage is an intense moss-green and the flower-buds appear months before they finally come into full bloom. This shrub prefers a lime-free soil, but I find I can put plants with these requirements in my rockery, where it is possible to make a pocket of the particular mixture needed for whatever is to be grown. In this way plants normally alien to the soil you have can be accommodated, with the surrounding rocks holding the specially made area firmly in place and not so liable to be washed away by heavy rain.

Luckily the *Erica carnea* group suit my garden perfectly and I grow a number of different colours. *E. carnea* 'Springwood White', and the 'Pink' as well, have flowers which contrast sharply with their dark green leaves, and if the bushes are trimmed with shears into a neat round shape after blooming they remain a solid hump and don't get straggly and untidy. *E. carnea* 'King George' is a good dark red, but I think the best, and my favourite, is *E. carnea* 'Vivellii' because in addition to the rich carmine flowers the foliage is a deep bronze and very striking.

Figure 4.8: *Erica carnea* 'Springwood White'

The trees which are the backbone of the winter garden, which began to flower in November, if not earlier, will still be putting out their pale pink blossoms this month and right into spring. The *Prunus subhirtella* 'Autumnalis' tends to wait for any mild sunny spell to put out its delicate sprays of flowers. But although the frost browns them and delays more buds opening, at the first rise in temperature and burst of sunshine, the tree is covered in blossom again, flowering along the leafless branches. My father planted three sizes of this prunus in my garden, a full tree, a standard and a half-standard. They are all round the house and at any time of the winter one of them is usually putting out some bloom.

But the viburnums, both *V. tinus* and *V.* × *bodnantense*, seem to take the cold in their stride and the latter's bright pink felty blooms come through the coldest winter in my garden quite undamaged. My tree is well over 12 ft high after twenty-five years, and the heady scent of the blooms gives me much pleasure — despite the fact that I have to struggle to hook back the garage door onto its post, long lost near the trunk of the tree. In summer, when the bright green heavily-veined leaves cover the branches, the occasional flowers it puts out from August onwards are not very visible, but the scent tells you they are there. *V. tinus* is evergreen and although originally from the Mediterranean region of Europe it seems to tolerate quite severe conditions and will grow in sun or shade. When it gets too large for its position in the garden, it can be cut to the ground and after one season will flower again and grow quickly into a rounded bush, hedge or tree; whatever seems best for the position you are growing it in. The pink-tinged white flowers have little scent though they are a decent size, but this viburnum also flowers for many months during the winter and for that reason is very good value.

I have found a good place for my favourite truly winter-flowering clematis, *C. cirrhosa* (*calycina*) *balearica* which has apple-green nodding bell-shaped flowers with purple anthers. I grow it up an *Acacia longifolia* in a corner of the house where its roots are protected and its evergreen bronze feathery leaves (it is known as the Fern-leaved Clematis) can climb up and show off the delicately-coloured blooms as and when they appear, discreetly framed by the dark foliage. For it will come into flower often in December and continue until March, and is hardy enough to stand a north aspect, as long as the roots are well covered. In summer the new growth of leaves are bright green.

Quite a number of the chaenomeles flower during winter. I much prefer the previous name of these plants, as *Cydonia* was the old name for these members of the quince family, which grew at Cydon in Crete, and these very tough shrubs, which are happy in sun or shade, are of the same genus as the true quince tree with its larger fruits, which was once far more commonly seen in gardens and the pear-shaped uniquely scented fruits used for preserves. Nevertheless, these ornamental shrubs do have much smaller fruits, following their various coloured flowers, and I make an astringent conserve from them for use as a pickle. These deciduous plants are very resistant to frost, only a prolonged air frost will cause any damage. When grown on a wall they need to be cut hard-back directly after flowering and when as a bush kept trimmed to a nice shape. The spurs which shoot successively after blooming can be trimmed two or three times in the season to keep the shrub in place, for flowers set on the old wood. In my own garden, after the blooming in January of C. × *superba* 'Pink Lady' under the protection of a wall, a 6 ft bush of C. *speciosa* 'Umbilicata' in the open border is covered in deep salmon-coloured cupped flowers. On the terrace steps the low-growing bushes of C. *speciosa* 'Rubra Grandiflora, which have been throwing out a few flowers all winter begin to open a mass of their large single crimson blooms, to make a fine and continuous display into March and April.

Cornus mas, the Cornelian Cherry, is a lovely shrub or small tree to come across when in flower as the tiny sulphur-yellow blossoms, shaped not unlike those of ceanothus, make a solid cloud of colour on the bare branches. The leaves, which appear later, turn a rich red in autumn; and in a good year and from a sheltered sunny position, the tree will bear fruits like rose-hips. As with the fruits of the arbutus, in southern Europe this cherry is used for cooking and made into jam. It can be grown as a standard tree — there is a very effective specimen on the lawn in the garden at Wadham College in Oxford; and a different growing of it as a large bush, with flowers to the ground, in a border there too. The cornus is happy in any soil and will grow to 20 ft high and almost as much across. A very basic ingredient of the winter flower garden and a pleasant sight at any time of the year.

The *Jasminum nudiflorum* will be at its best now, though it flowers very freely all through the winter, doing very well on a cheerless north wall. Whenever the blooms are not quite out, the green stems can be picked for the house, where the buds will quickly open. When grown as a bush this jasmine seems to do best when fairly heavily pruned by removing all the shoots that have flowered, and then it will be a solid mass of yellow the following year. When growing against a wall it will reach at least 15 ft so pruning can be done just to keep the plant neatly in its position. Next month the tender evergreen *Jasminum primulinum* (*mesnyi*) will follow on with its flowering, so that for more than half the year it is possible to have a yellow jasmine out, in the garden.

The Winter Sweet is a good name for this very strong-smelling shrub which we have been able to enjoy for over two hundred years, since it was introduced from China in 1766. *Chimonanthus praecox* has pale yellow claw-like flowers with maroon inner segments. It grows most freely against a wall with plenty of sun to ripen the wood. Even then it does not flower for six or seven years, but, I think, is well worth waiting for. It is such an easy plant to grow on any soil, doing particularly well on chalk, and is very hardy — the waxy flowers seem quite impervious to frost, rain or snow.

Figure 4.9: *Cornus mas*

The best way to propagate seems to be by layering in May. Eventually an old plant will reach 8-10 ft and will begin to flower as early as November and continue until February. The only pruning necessary is the removal of dead wood to encourage new growth when against a wall, and long pieces can be cut for the house when shaping a bush, and will fill a room with their heady perfume. There is a larger variety, *C. praecox* 'Grandiflorus', but the scent is not so pungent and another variety, *C. praecox* 'Luteus', is later blooming and the flowers lack the striking chocolaty centres which make the plant so unusual. As with many plants a new variety may be better in some ways, but sometimes a particular attribute of the original is lost.

To follow on the *Camellia sasanquas*, which may have first bloomed as early as November, the *Camellia × williamsii* hybrids will be flowering on and off through the winter, being at their best, usually, in February. There are about two dozen different varieties, all a cross between *C. japonica* and *C. saluenensis* and they are in flower over many weeks and have the great advantage of dropping their dead blooms, unlike the *C. japonica* bushes which tend to look rather untidy. The three best known and most reliable are *C. × williamsii*, 'Bow Bells', 'Donation' and 'J.C. Williams'. They all have different forms of flower and are various shades of pink. Unfortunately they have no scent like the *C. sasanqua* kinds, but they will flower as far north as Scotland, which even the *C. japonica* variety will not. Camellias make a very good hedge and can be clipped hard to shape after flowering with secateurs or even shears, as is the custom in Portugal and Spain. But they also grow well against a wall, particularly the tall-growing varieties, and if the soil is not ideal in your garden, they do well in a pot in a special ericaceous mixture; but care is needed that they do not dry out. Alternatively the ground can be specially prepared with acid compost, peat and sand. I think pots are a way of having plants you like and want in the garden that your soil does not suit; but it does make for more work; I am constantly doing the finger test for soil dryness and frequently watering my numerous pots, but I find it just worthwhile, and useful to be able to move a flowering tub to a place in the garden that may, at that moment, be bare of flower, and so produce instant colour for that aspect.

Two rhododendrons which are, usually, in full flower in February are *R.* 'Praecox' and *R. moupinense*. The first is useful as it will tolerate a little lime in the soil unlike most other rhododendrons. The glossy leaves are fragrant when crushed and usually remain on the bush throughout the year, though the plant can occasionally become deciduous. It makes a small graceful bush growing between 2-4 ft so it is not too big for the rockery and is a sun lover, lasting in flower several weeks, the lilac flowers making such a good contrast against the dark green leaves. *R. moupinense* is another dwarf-growing plant with scaly undersides to the dark oval leaves. But the flowers are larger than *R.* 'Praecox' being white with crimson markings and with a very pleasant scent. As they can be 2 in

Figure 4.10: View of garden with *Camellia* × *williamsii* 'Bow Bells' in foreground

across, they are not so frost or wind resistant as those of the little lilac one, but with some shelter I think the plant is well worth growing, to have the reward of seeing the loose clusters of snowy flowers so much earlier than the main blooming of the larger rhododendrons.

Iris reticulata is a little bulbous iris with deep violet flowers and distinctive gold marks on the falls. It grows well in the rockery in a sunny position, preferring a light soil. The leaves are unusual, as they are four-sided. I saw a very effective planting recently on a grassy bank, where serried ranks of these iris in varieties of colour, from reddish-purple to palest blue, made a bright carpet against the snow-covered ground.

The Algerian Iris, *Iris stylosa*, now known by the cumbersome name *I. unguicularis*, gives a lovely mass of flowers during winter, particularly if the rhizomes have been baked in the summer by being planted half out of the soil. The leaves make a large untidy clump and if left untouched I find snails hide away and eat the flowers as they struggle up out of the foliage. In autumn I cut the leaves down, after their summer baking and then the flowers stand clear of the base when they bloom, making their peak showing in February. Should they be required for the house, the flower-stems should be pulled, not cut, when still looking like a tight tube. They will then gradually unfurl in the house and last longer than when picked fully out. There are various colours other than the type, which is lavender-blue with an orange stripe towards the base of each petal. Someone has given me a miniature variety from Crete (*I. cretensis*) and I have also planted a deep blue form from the shores of the Black Sea named *I. lazica*. A white variety is rare and expensive, but some half-a-dozen different kinds of this iris, which will give flowers over many weeks, are available from specialist nurseries and are well worth tracking down. Once planted at the foot of a sunny wall or fence, they need very little attention, as they don't mind being dried out as well as baked.

Another small bulbous iris to flower now is *I. danfordiae*, 3-4 in tall, with soft yellow blooms, the falls speckled brown. After flowering the bulbs break up and it is difficult to get them to bloom the following season unless they are planted very deeply — around 9 in or more — so that they do not get dispersed by injudicious hoeing during the non-flowering time, and before the bulblets have had time to mature. They also prefer a sandy soil and a good feed of bonemeal at the end of the summer will encourage them to throw up shoots. But it is wise to plant a few fresh bulbs every year to make sure of having the cheerful sight of pale yellow so early in the season.

From a similar area of the world as the *Iris stylosa* come the winter-flowering cyclamen, of which the main group are *C. coum* with deep carmine flowers and darker marking at the base of the tiny petal. They are thought to have originated from the Greek island of Kos, but have not been found there recently. *C. coum roseum* is of a paler shade, but the one I think lights up the winter scene is *C. coum album*, because the pure white

Figure 4.11: _Cyclamen coum_

flowers are enhanced by the distinctive crimson zone at the petal base. The corms grow happily in a woodland setting, particularly if they can benefit from the fall from deciduous trees to feed their roots; and they will increase over the years to make a drift of colour. The seeds are also carried round the garden by insects or birds, for I have little clumps in different corners, which appear unexpectedly and add much to the numerous surprises of gardening.

The forest tree of the Himalayas _Magnolia campbellii_ or the Pink Tulip Tree, has the most magnificent flowers which can be up to 10 in across and give off soft scent from the deep pink blooms, paler within. Because it flowers so early in the year and grows to as much as 60 ft, it must be planted in those parts of the country where the flowers can be protected from the cold. The drawback is, it does not flower for about twenty years, but the waiting time is well rewarded. There is a fine example of this tree growing in a garden at Salcombe in South Devon. The garden is terraced so that, although the tree is about 50 ft high, you can lean over a wall and look at the superb cup-shaped blooms at close quarters and catch the faint scent they exude. So the exotic flowers are, unusually, at eye-level and can be enjoyed to the full. If you are not prepared to wait so long for this beautiful tree, there are various hybrids which have been produced to flower as early as ten years, and a container-grown plant several years old, though more expensive, will cut the time down again to a reasonable limit. For the majority of people nowadays are not willing or able to stay in one garden long enough to see the flowering of one of the world's finest trees. And, of course, most gardens are not large enough to accommodate such a grand specimen; but anyone can have much pleasure from the flowering in a few weeks' time, in March, of the comparatively diminutive, but striking *Magnolia stellata*.

Most of the gromwells or lithospermums bloom in the spring and summer, the most well known, *L. diffusum* 'Heavenly Blue', often carrying the odd flower well into winter. But it has a disadvantage because it is only happy in acid soil, whereas the true winter-flowering *L. rosmarinifolium* will thrive in any neutral ground, and produces in January and February bright blue flowers — the buds are intriguingly tinged with pink — on a rounded shrub with narrow green leaves, and it will reach several feet square in a favoured site. This variety seems to be able to stand the cold very well as long as it is kept fairly dry. It is a plant that hails from southern Italy and can be seen growing on limestone cliffs in Capri. It will make a blaze of blue in the very bleakest time of the year even in this country. Tucked into a sheltered nook of the rock garden it will then give of its best, and in favoured areas grow into a little shrub. Otherwise it can be grown in a pot and plunged outdoors in the summer and then put in a greenhouse or on a window-sill to flower all winter.

Helleborus foetidus, a native plant but rare in the wild these days, come into bloom about now, and although the flowers are a similar colour but a lighter green than the leaves, it will grow in total shade, so is a useful plant for a dank corner and is not as unpleasant-smelling as its name suggests. The flowers are attractive on a dull winter's day, being bright green and edged with maroon. This helleborus remains in flower for many weeks, so it is good value in the winter garden and lights up a dark spot. It is a shrubby helleborus, holding its leaves until fresh appear, when the old ones can be removed.

A very distinctive snowdrop which made an unexpected but welcome appearance in my rockery a few years ago is one of the taller kinds, *Galanthus elwesii*. It chose its spot well for that part of the rockery is in full sun and this variety comes from Turkey, and therefore appreciates all the light we can provide here. The flowers have a more globular shape than the common snowdrop, which will have flowered earlier in January, and beneath the glistening-white petals the cleft and the base of the inner segments are coloured bright green. Most of the species do not like to be

Figure 4.12: *Magnolia campbellii*

Figure 4.13: *Helleborus foetidus*

too dry, or to have very much sand in the soil, but otherwise they are easy to naturalise under shrubs and trees as well as in rockeries and flower-beds. *G. whittallii* is a sub-species of *G. elwesii*, but even taller and more elegant.

Bergenias have a romantic-sounding name and were once a great favourite in cottage gardens. Their leaves are generously rounded or heart-shaped, with the very vivid nickname of 'elephant ears', and the plants give a lush appearance whether they are grouped in a clump in the border or rock garden, or grown *en masse* when the green- to purple-coloured leaves make a dramatic contrast to other plant leaves nearby.

There are five species of bergenia with various hybrids and cultivars. Linnaeus, the Swedish botanist, whose flower listing is the basis of all modern naming, placed these plants under *Saxifraga*; then they were known as *Megasea* and can still be found under this name in old books. But now they are always known and listed as *Bergenias*.

Figure 4.14: *Bergenia delavayi*

I have several plants with rich-green, slightly fleshy leaves, and at the turn of the year they begin to put out new shoots and by February the pink flower trusses are unfurling. They ascend from the centre of the plant as a rounded knot of buds and as they bloom the flower-head arises on its stem clear of the mound of leaves and remains so for several weeks, the pink gradually fading and browning till they are 'blown' as is said about flowers past their best.

These plants will grow in some shade though they look very imposing with the sun shining on the handsome leaves, which in some varieties are mahogany-purple. The flowers range in colour from white through pink to red and purple, and at heights of a few inches to a foot or more.

My plants have been in the garden many years and I bought them as *B. delavayi* — now grouped with *B. purpurascens*. I have been advised now by an expert that they are *B. schmidtii* but I am not entirely convinced, for the latter flowers in the autumn as well as February, and I cannot recall any of my plants, tucked protectively away at the top of the rockeries, ever showing any of their bright pink flowers till February.

I believe a whole bed of these plants, incorporating the different colours and size of leaf and flower, would make a magnificent winter display; and the massed, impressively large leaves could be made a feature and would still give a very fine background to other plants and beds in the garden during the rest of the year.

I am not very fond of tulips because the often-present wind in my garden on the coast means a mass of flattened plants like collapsed soldiers before they have had time to open their buds. But fortunately the first tulip to flower is low-growing and made of tougher stuff. The Water Lily Tulip, *Tulipa kaufmanniana*, opens its petals wide, partly within the protection of the long glaucous leaves. It has large blooms with pointed petals, creamy-white strengthening to yellow at the base of the flower, and the outside of the petals are pink-striped. But there are various other colours including all scarlet, a pure white touched with red, a suffused pale rose and the well-known *T. kaufmanniana* 'Shakespeare' which is salmon and apricot. These tulips in their brilliant hues like to be planted in a position where they can be baked by the sun in summer, just as they are in Turkestan in the USSR where they were first found. They increase by making bulbs below the original, so if you do lift them, dig well below for the dropper — that is a shoot leading down from the main bulb to make a new one. They are easy to grow, but do prefer the soil to be on the calcareous side, and are quite happy to be left in the ground all year, unlike the ordinary tulip which is better lifted in summer and re-planted in the autumn.

There are so many attractive miniature daffodils. Though dwarf in height some have quite large flowers, while others are real teenies in every way, and all look enchanting in little groups in a rockery. I grow them also in clumps around a tulip tree in a circular bed which is a mass of roses in summer, but in winter the bright yellow carpet under the bare, heavily pruned rose branches gives the bed a double, and all year round, use. I have *Crocus ancyrensis* immediately round the stem of the tulip tree, then *Tulipa kaufmanniana* in an outer circle, and beyond these, collective plantings of around half-a-dozen bulbs of *Narcissus* 'Tête-a-tête', and the dear little miniature *Tulipa pulchella humilis* with pink blooms and then following on a little later *T. pulchella violacea* whose flowers are purple-violet. These tulips are only 5 in tall and such bright neat surprises. The whole bed is ringed by a low box edging I am growing round the circumference.

One of the cheeriest sights, easily visible from the windows of my sitting-room — a vital requisite of winter flower planting — is the early daffodil *Narcissus cyclamineus* 'February Gold' with its bright gold corona and paler yellow perianth. It seems to be increasing happily in the moist peaty soil I have between the rockery stones.

Figure 4.15: *Tulipa kaufmanniana*

By February, too, the *Primula polyanthus* will be in full flower. They are often grown very effectively massed in beds, but I like them dotted about under the winter shrubs in groups of two or three, drawing the eye with their vivid hues. The range of their colour, often with a contrasting centre, means they will complement whatever plant is nearby. Little pots of them can be bought at any nursery or even a greengrocer — or grown easily from seed — and once planted they settle down and become part of the flowering pattern of the garden in winter. They can be propagated by division in mid-summer, but they seem to bloom better when raised from seed, though they take a little longer before the first blossoms appear. Of all the colours, the large-flowered and sweetly scented 'Barrowby Gem' with golden-yellow blooms takes a lot of beating.

Many of these plants will flower over the whole period of the winter months, like the *Prunus subhirtella* 'Autumnalis', the *Viburnum tinus* and *Jasminum nudiflorum*; and others such as the *Chimonanthus praecox*, the *Viburnum* × *bodnantense* and the *Lonicera fragrantissima* giving off, in addition, their sweet scent. Then as February comes to an end and the flush of bloom carries on into March, and its first fortnight brings to a close the time I count as winter, they will all meet and overlap with the flowers of spring.

Chapter 5

March

In March the days stretch long and light, yet it often lets me down as a month for its promises are not always fulfilled. The warming sun brings the plants on, but the winds can be blustery and chill, and with the equinox approaching, the weather is rarely to be relied on from one day to the next. Still, though spring may be delayed, there are many plants that flower in the first two weeks of March, sometimes starting a little earlier or holding back for a few days, depending on the prevailing set-up in the sky. And these all bring my winter-flowering garden time to its completion, though of course at both ends of the span that I count as winter, there are masses of blooms hung over from summer and beginning their spring, that make these two periods a particularly flower-packed time of the year.

Following on all the beautiful daphnes which were in flower by last month, a rather more unusual one, *D. blagayana*, will come into bloom now, but it does appreciate special treatment. Unlike *D. odora* and *D. mezereum*, which will tolerate any soil, *D. blagayana* needs a leafy soil and plenty of limestone. It grows low to the ground, as the branches fan out from the main stem, and if these branches are pegged down beneath rocks, the bunches of creamy-white flowers at each terminal are held steady. They are surrounded by a rosette of shining green leaves, giving the effect of a Victorian posy. The buried section will root and can be separated later to make another plant. The scent from this intriguing variety is the strongest of all, I think, and the flowers being low to the ground, the fragrance hangs about, and a further advantage is that the whole plant is less easily damaged by wind and can be quickly covered in severe weather. There are daphnes to suit every soil and situation, which will give flower from February to August that I know of, some deciduous, some evergreen. Most of them have this delicious perfume, so making them, especially in the winter, a real joy for the garden and I think a top priority when planting, however small the area you have at your disposal.

Figure 5.1: *Daphne blagayana*

All winter the tough deciduous *Jasminum nudiflorum* has been throwing out its sprays of yellow flowers, but now in March, if a warm south-facing wall gives sufficient protection, it is well worth trying to grow *J. mesnyi* also known as *J. primulinum*. This has still brighter yellow flowers, twice the size and half-double with a delicate orange marking in the centre and, as its name implies, reminiscent of a primrose. These bloom against the ever-green three-leaved sprays of foliage. This plant, unlike the *J. nudiflorum*, has proper climbing stems, and was brought back from Yunnan, a province of China, by the plant collector Ernest Wilson. It will hug a warm brick wall, growing at least 15 ft high and as much across. I first saw a striking plant of this jasmine spreading along a great wall in the Chelsea Physic Garden in London (the second oldest Botanic garden in England and founded in 1673, the first in the world being set up in Pisa, Italy, in 1543), and fortunately they had little plants for sale and now I have mine tucked into a southern corner against the white wall of my house. I am glad I took the trouble to bring it home as I now learn this variety is difficult to set from seed. And I do grow a lot of my shrubs from seed nowadays, as plants become more expensive; and somehow it means more to you and is terribly exciting when the particular plant you desire develops from seed as opposed to a cutting. A magical thing arising out of the soil. But to be practical, many plants are far more successful taken from cuttings and placed in a mixture consisting principally of sharp sand, peat and a little soil.

But absolutely no trouble to grow and probably the most well-known anemone is the Poppy Anemone, *A. coronaria*, with its cup-shaped flowers of every shade of colour except yellow. They are tuberous rooted and like a sunny site in well-drained soil, as they come from the Mediterranean region. There are single flowers named 'St Brigid' and semi-double called 'de Caen' and, like the *A. pulsatilla* group, they have a frilly collar just below the bloom which adds to their charm. Their leaves are delicate finely-cut sprays. The knobbly little tubers should be planted in September, about 2 in deep and then they will come into flower in March and can be left in place for years, when they gradually seem to appear earlier each season; several have flowered in my garden, recently, in December.

Another group of anemones which used to be known as *A. hepatica*, but are now called *Hepatica nobilis*, are in varying shades of blue, red, pink and also white and at 6 in in height, both single and double, make wonderful drifts of colour amid their three-cornered lobed leaves, in the shade side of the rock garden or rough woodland. Another, rather difficult one to get established, is a little alpine species *A. vernalis* with violet goblet-shaped blooms dusted with yellow hairs which, among its fine-cut green leaves, open to a pure white perched on 3 in stems. But if happily placed it will flower during the winter months, and confirm its name 'The Lady of the Snows'; and seed collected in July will propagate very easily, once you have persuaded this anemone to bloom well.

A. fulgens shows by its colour that it comes from Greece, that country of such intense light. The brilliant scarlet petals with a centre of black anthers need plenty of sun and a hot dry site to give of their best. It is a perennial and the 10 in stems make a good plant for cutting to cheer the room on a dull day. And in the rock garden it stands out with its sharp colour and complements all the other flowers blooming there at this time.

What good value flowers the anemone gives. From the graceful tall deep pink to white blooms of the summer-flowering Japanese varieties, to the *A. pulsatillas* of spring with their purple, red or white cups with Elizabethan-like ruffs of green fringing the globular cups of furry stems. As early as December I have known *A. blanda* to open its starry little mauve, blue, pink or white flowers and as these go over in late February and March *A. hepatica* (*Hepatica nobilis*) takes over, growing like a clump of primroses, with similar colours to the *A. blanda* but producing the double as well as single flowers. *A. blanda* — the best colour is, I think, the deep-blue *atrocoerulea* — will naturalise very well, seeding itself, and looks lovely left to grow wild in grass among trees. I like to see it in my winter rockery, where it blends nicely and makes a good colour group with little treasures like the early primroses, snowdrops and cyclamen.

One of these I find very choice is the *Muscari botryoides album*, the dazzling white form of the blue Grape Hyacinth, *M. botryoides*. There is also a pale blue one, half the height of these two, *M. azureum*, but I want to plant a rare 10 in purple-brown form, *M. moschatum major*, which turns yellow with age, but has a very definite scent of musk. I don't believe any of the other forms of grape hyacinth have such a fragrance and the colours sound unusual. Muscari are very easy to grow, and look best, I find, in the rockery in a sunny position, but are alright tucked under a small deciduous plant.

One of the smallest magnolias, which has the additional benefit of flowering when young, even though it is slow growing, is *M. stellata*. It very seldom exceeds 10 ft in height decades after planting and so is the best one to have where space is limited. The partly double narrow-petalled flowers are glistening white and slightly fragrant, opening from furry grey buds which protect well from any frost. There is a pink variety, *M. stellata* 'Rosea', and a richer colour, *M. stellata* 'Rubra', but the finest form from Japan is *M. stellata* 'Water Lily', with even larger white flowers massed over the entire bush. When my magnolia blooms I know Easter-time is near, and spring not so far behind.

Tucked underneath my bay-window, because it only grows 2-3 ft high, is what I think is the most spectacular colour of the cydonias or chaeno-meles. This is *C. speciosa* 'Simonii' with stunning blood-red flowers partially double. I have found them completely resistant to the hardest of frosts. There are nine different bushes of cydonia in my garden, on the terrace steps, against the fence, grown on the white walls of the house or as a free-standing shrub pruned into a 6 ft dome shape; and they have all

Figure 5.2:
Anemone blanda

prospered, never showing any signs of collapse or of dying on me. They are careless as to what type of soil they grow in or in what position, and will tolerate lime and seem particularly happy on my heavy clay soil, and in the worst areas of it too. What a pity the flowers have no scent. But, apart from this, they all give very good value in decorating the garden with their blooms, producing them spasmodically at all times of the year.

There are two forsythias that flower during the winter period and their differing habits make them a nice contrasting pair to grow together. The first, *F. giraldiana*, makes a spreading bush of slender branches hung with primrose-yellow scented bell-shaped blooms. The one I have is *F. ovata* which is very compact and slow growing with flowers of a deeper chrome-yellow. I prune it to shape immediately after flowering so that it will not obscure or tangle with an old camellia growing next to it. They make a nice pair and lighten a dark slope of the garden with their golden and crimson blooms. The camellia is *C. japonica* 'Campbellii' which I planted twenty years ago and in the ensuing years this variety has disappeared from many of the catalogues. It has a charming little flower, semi-double and a true scarlet. They cover the plant and contrast well with the glossy green leaves, and the forsythia beside it which has bare twiggy branches clothed with the amber clusters. The soil is fine for the forsythia and as there are overhead deciduous trees there must be enough leaf-mould to keep the camellia happy and level out the basic clay content. The slope of course means good drainage and the shrubs get enough sun to ripen the wood and set the flowers, whereas evergreens overhead would preclude this. I do put peat and compost round the plants once or twice a year to give an extra feed and to encourage them, and they certainly make a great display, in return, in early March.

I mourn the loss of a rather rare shrub I once had, *Edgeworthia chrysantha* also known as *E. papyrifera*, a shrub from China related to the daphne with clusters of pendant tubular yellow flowers with a scent of spice, and dark green narrow leaves. My shrub eventually grew tall enough so that you could stand next to it under the intriguingly fragrant blooms, which in a mild year come into flower in February, but certainly by early March. The pliable willowy stems carry the bunches of scented flowers at their tips, covered in cobwebby hairs. For many years my edgeworthia seemed quite happy and grew well, but I believe a particularly hard winter killed it and I should have given it more shelter; it was in a border near a fence, but open to the prevailing westerly gales. When I find another plant it will merit a warmer corner site, for it is a desirable and showy acquisition and possesses the strong scent of so many winter flowers.

Most of the pieris shrubs flower too late to be included in the winter garden, but there is one, the hardiest and most vigorous in growth of the genus, *P. japonica* 'Christmas Cheer'. In a mild year this will flower in time to live up to its name, but I find it is often March before the bush is at its best, when it makes a very colourful picture with its serrated oval leaves, glossy and green against the clusters of pitcher-like flowers tinged with pink. The flowers are very like those of lily-of-the-valley, and similar to arbutus blooms. Pieris has unusual colouring in that the young leaf shoots are tinted bronze, so that when combined with the old green foliage and the pinky-white flowers, it makes quite an effect in the garden. It needs a sheltered site in a moist lime-free soil, and some shade. And when planting, the surround and background need to be considered so that the plant will display itself in the most dramatic way. And an added bonus would be a site visible from the house.

To complement the bulbous-rooted plant *Sternbergia lutea* and the other varieties flowering around November, there is the slightly taller-growing *S. fischeriana* that produces its blooms at the same time as the strap-like leaves, unlike *S. lutea* which flowers before the leaves appear. They like to be set deep in warm leafy neutral soil and in a position where they can be baked by the summer sun. *S. fischeriana*, with its sharp-yellow goblets, needs planting in July or August whereas the early winter-flowering kinds should be planted in April. They all do best if lifted every three years and divided. They make lovely groups in the garden, opening their larger-than-crocus-shaped blooms to the sun in a mass of yellow.

A very attractive variation on the *Prunus subhirtella* 'Autumnalis', which has been flowering on and off all through the winter, is *P. subhirtella* 'Pendula Rubra' which in March produces deep rose-red single flowers massed along its arching stems, so that a well-trained tree will be covered to the ground making an umbrella of dark pink blossom. Alternatively, it can be grown at the top of the rockery, and trained to weep its rose-madder covered branches over the boulders, but kept within bounds by pruning; a specially graceful bush or tree with a habit and colour that is always appealing.

The vanilla scent of the *Azara microphylla* comes from little yellow clusters of stamens, the flowers having no petals. This variety makes a graceful small tree with fern-like branches of green, glossy leaves. Two other kinds flower at the end of winter, *A. integrifolia* and *A. petiolaris* and the latter is particularly hardy. I had a 20 ft high shrub which quite outgrew its place near the front door, but this flowered in spring and its leaves were often blackened by cold wind and frost. This one was *A. dentata*, with heavily scented puffs of yellow flowers. They are not shrubs you see growing in many gardens; I first noticed one covering the outer wall of the lion house at a zoo in a very mild part of the country, and I asked the keeper for a cutting. It is sad my huge bush died of what appeared to be honey-fungus, but before it finally succumbed I had been able to take various cuttings myself to grow on in the garden and the one I gave to my neighbour is now 6 ft sq in a fairly exposed position. So these plants from Chile are worth looking for and they flower well in winter, which approximates to spring in their native home.

Another larger tree, *Parrotia persica*, the Iron Tree or Persian Witch

Hazel, grows up to 30 ft and has a spreading shape rather like a beech tree. It has small red clusters of stamens along the bare branches in late winter which open from woolly buds. Like other witch hazels the leaves turn scarlet and yellow before they fall. The parrotia needs training when young to a good shape as it likes to grow out horizontally; though there is a form *P. persica* 'Pendula' which allows it to develop in the way it prefers.

The *Osmaronia cerasiformis*, the Oso Berry, also known as *Nuttallia cerasiformis* after the American botanist Thomas Nuttall, who discovered it, is easy to grow in any soil and produces greenish-white flowers, with a scent of almond, which hang from the erect suckering stems in February or March. In the summer the bush is loaded with oblong fruits, having the bloom and colour of a purple plum, set among elliptic grey-tinged leaves.

The osmanthus, though having a slightly similar name, are evergreen shrubs which come mainly from China. *O. heterophyllus*, I have mentioned, does flower in November but *O. delavayi*, with its dainty dark green leaves and fragrant ivory tubular flowers does not scent my rockery until April. However, there are three varieties that flower earlier in the year. The first, *O. suavis*, is related to *O. delavayi* but needs a sheltered position as it flowers between December and March and has much larger spear-like leaves from glandular stems, but the flowers are just as strongly perfumed and very noticeable in the cold air. Then *O. yunnanensis* has olive-green leaves twice the size of those of *O. suavis* and will grow in a short time to make a small tree. A slower developing variety is *O. serrulatus* from the Himalayas with shiny-green slim and serrated leaves, and from the axils comes the sweet scent of the pure-white flowers. I think this last one is the best to grow, only reaching 4 ft sq eventually and flowering through February and March.

The fritillaria is a bulb that in its varieties mostly flowers in the spring, but there are one or two rare and rather expensive ones that produce their blooms earlier and can be obtained from specialist nurseries. *F. recurva* has stems of 12 in and bears nodding bells of scarlet and orange speckled flowers of much charm. The bulbs like a sandy peaty soil, very well-drained, and to be kept much drier than the later flowering *F. meleagris*, and to be baked hard in summer, only watering whilst growing. *F. pudica* is, as its name implies, a modest little flower barely 6 in high with bright yellow flowers. It comes from western America and is the only American fritillaria to resemble those from the Mediterranean. Other March flowering bulbs to look for are *F. bucharica* from the Caucasus with white flowers tinted green and *F. oranensis* whose blooms are rich purple, and *F. schleimannii* from west Turkey with sea-green flowers. One of each of these bulbs planted in a sunny spot would make an uncommon little group and a real talking-point in the garden. Each individual bulb could be increased later by scaling, so even though expensive, it is only necessary to buy one of each to start with.

The Dog's Tooth Violet is so-called because of the shape of the bulb,

Figure 5.3:
Erythronium citrinum

but *Erythronium dens-canis* is not like a violet in flower either, the cyclamen-type blooms are 2 in across and the 6 in high bulbous-rooted plants have elegant mottled leaves. They like light sandy soil and a mulch of leaf-mould or peat, as they do not like to be dry and will form pretty clumps in grass in a wild woodland area, as long as it is not too shaded, and look remarkably good in the rock garden. *E. dens-canis*, which comes from Europe and Asia, has pink, lavender or white flowers and *E. citrinum* is an early-flowering yellow variety and *E.* 'Franz Hals' a clear purple-rose. But there are some lovely species from North America, particularly *E. mesochoreum* from Kansas and Iowa, with soft lavender flowers only 5 in high, and one with a beautiful shape and a rich deep pink shade *E. revolutum johnsonii* 'Rose Beauty', and *E. revolutum* 'White Beauty' a white with a cream throat; but these last two don't often flower till April, so are not within the winter flower garden range, but make a nice follow-on.

Another plant for wild areas of light woodland is a form of the Periwinkle, *Vinca difformis*, which flowers any sunny day in winter and can be kept in order in a dull corner of a bed by secateuring the leaders that throw themselves out everywhere and make the ordinary form, particularly, of this pretty plant (*V. major* or *V. minor*) such a trial in the garden; for it spreads so fast and the roots become very invasive. But *V. difformis* has delicately pale mauve blooms and *V. difformis dubia* from Algeria is a deeper colour. As one of my favourite old gardening books says rather disparagingly, 'these may be used to cover any worthless corner'. The flowers are so charming I feel they should be better treated than that, but, nevertheless, very firmly handled and controlled.

My *Mahonia japonica* is at its best in March, though it has thrown out a few sprays of its pale yellow scented flowers for months, accompanying the two Chinese varieties, first the *M. lomariifolia* in November, and then *M. bealei* in February. But now its rounded buds open fully to the lighter days and the 10 in long slender racemes of flower vie with the huge pinnate leaves of deep green touched with bronze, gradually developing into a large handsome bush and giving off a heady sweet perfume. Like the berberis, to which they are related, mahonias grow in any soil but like sun to ripen the wood, for the flowers, and purple-black berries which follow; these are edible, certainly by the birds. The very large-leaved kinds need some shelter to preserve them from the wind.

There is an enchanting little plant from the ranunculus species *R. calandrinioides* that will flower in February and March in the garden if tucked into a warm sheltered spot in neutral soil. It grows 6 in tall with grey-green leaves like spears and usually with pale pink single blooms and conspicuous yellow stamens; sometimes the flowers can be white with a faint rosy tinge on their backs. It is an herbaceous plant, dying down to the root annually, but as it flowers in the cold time of the year here, and comes from North Africa, it does need careful protected siting and would not survive in bleak northern areas out of doors.

Another tender little treasure is the Chilean blue crocus *Tecophilaea cyanocrocus* with the most intense blue flower, with white markings like the strokes of a paint-brush at the throat. The plants are barely 4 in high so are very subject to slug damage. The leaves are slender and glossy. There is a pale blue, *T. cyanocrocus leichtlinii*, and a violet, *T. cyanocrocus violacea*, but the type is I think the most desirable to have for the wonderful depth of its blue colour. As with other rare and expensive bulbs a start can be made with a single bulb and if cosseted in a sunny position in light sandy soil it should thrive, and then offsets from this bulb will, in time, produce a little colony and the sight of them all eventually in flower will be well worth the waiting and labour involved.

The March-flowering rhododendrons are fairly numerous and precede the full blooming of the main species in the spring. If you have the space in your garden a very fine tree is *R. barbatum* which comes from the Himalayas and will grow from 6-30 ft in time, the finest reaching as much as 60 ft with the main stem about a foot across. The large evergreen leaves and the blood-red flowers in March require the protection of a woodland garden. Coming down to earth, the *R.* 'Christmas Cheer' grows only a few feet high and accommodates nicely into any size plot. The pink buds are rarely open till March, for when it was given its name the plant was probably grown in a greenhouse, as camellias were years ago. The fully opened flowers gradually pale to the faintest rose, and remain out for several weeks. Another very neat little bush I have is *R. cilpinense* a cross between *R. ciliatum* and *R. moupinense*, the latter having flowered last month. This cross has snow-white flowers with a hint of pink in the bud. The leaves are very dark green and tiny, compared with the huge size of the *R. barbatum*. Another choice March flowerer is *R. lutescens*, a good contrast to the others with clear lemon clusters of funnel-like blooms and pointed narrow leaves which have touches of red.

These early rhododendrons need shelter from cold winds and from the midday sun in summer. As long as they have well-drained soil with plenty of peat and compost added they will thrive, but do not want to be planted near other shallow-rooters, such as chestnuts and beeches, which will take their nourishment and dry them out. Cherries and laburnums have deep roots and will not interfere with the surface roots of the rhododendrons. My *R.* 'Christmas Cheer' seems happy near a tall open cistus bush, with a fence nearby to mitigate the prevailing wind, which would certainly tear at the papery flowers.

Liking a semi-shaded position, too, are the pulmonarias, the so-called lungworts, because they were once used to treat diseases of the lung (pulmo). These are completely hardy herbaceous perennials with hairy stems which mostly begin to flower in April and May. But several species do bloom earlier and make good patches of colour tucked into crevices in the rock garden. There are four nicely contrasting shades, all from continental Europe, the first *P. angustifolia* happy in any soil whereas the others

Figure 5.4: *Scilla bifolia*

prefer a neutral one. The flowers are deep purple-blue, the variety *P. angustifolia azurea* of a lighter, but a lovely bright gentian blue. *P. montana*, also known as *P. rubra*, has wider leaves and salmon-red blooms, *P. saccharata*, the Bethlehem Sage, has leaves spotted with white and pink flowers which change to blue as they age, so giving the effective sight of both colours on the same plant at once, against the green and white marbled leaves. There are two new forms of the *P. saccharata*, 'Sissinghurst White' and 'Bowles Red' and this gives an even wider range of colour for these easily grown plants.

Three late winter-flowering bulbs all closely related to each other are the scillas, the chionodoxas and puschkinias. The scillas, or squills, like limy soil and *S. sibirica* has bright blue flowers hanging like bells on 6 in stems about three to every bulb. *S. bifolia* is a little shorter with six-petalled flowers and I also have a rather pretty pink one, *S. bifolia rosea*. *S. tubergeniana*, from Iran, is the palest blue with a darker stripe, numerous blooms opening gradually on the stems. These bulbous plants prefer a sunny spot but will grow in half-shade.

The chionodoxa or Glory of the Snow has similar flowers but they look upwards instead of hanging down and *C. luciliae* has a white throat to its starry blue flower. Again there is a good contrasting pink, *C. luciliae rosea*. I would like to have a rather rare one from Crete, barely 4 in high, *C. nana* with pale lilac blooms; all ideal for the rockery. And from the Lebanon comes a similar bulbous rooted plant, allied to the scilla, and named after the Russian botanist who found it, M. Pouschkin and known as *Puschkinia scilloides*, the striped squill. This has blue-white flowers thickly clustered on the stem rather like the form of *Scilla tubergeniana*. It likes neutral soil and an open sunny position.

Among these little groups more clumps of ericas will be flowering as March begins. *E. carnea* 'Ruby Glow' has rich bronze leaves and large flowers, the glowing colour of its name. The *carnea* group, also known as *E. herbacea*, are so versatile; unlike many of the heaths, which must have an acid peaty soil to do well, this mountain one will tolerate a limy soil, but not very shallow chalk. They also make marvellous ground cover, planted about 10 in apart and sheared to a tight bunch after flowering; then in a few years they will completely join up and make a kaleidoscope of colour, as the different varieties come into flower, the permanent solid background of green foliage deterring all weeds.

A bulb known as the Spring Star Flower, which comes from South America, is the ipheion and white trumpets open flat and lie like stars against the fine-cut leaves; this white variety, *I. uniflorum*, is washed with blue shades, but *I. uniflorum* 'Wisley Blue' is, I think, the nicest form, being a strong violet-blue, and it will flower in February or March with me, when the weather has not been too severe, and it is planted to catch the warming winter sun. The flowers and leaves smell faintly of garlic when crushed.

Figure 5.5: *Chionodoxa luciliae*

Adonis, the Flower of the Gods, is a perennial in its winter form, the bud appearing from the soil and opening its anemone-like golden blooms in late February or early March. *A. amurensis*, from the Amur River in Siberia, has single 2 in flowers set among feathery foliage and there is a pretty double variety *A. amurensis fl. pl.* and another, also double, *A. wolgensis* with green tips to the petals. These rise about 10 in from the ground, but *A. vernalis* is perhaps the choicest, being barely 6 in high, with even larger flowers.

The Japanese use the adonis as a special flower in the house on New Year's Day and through their interest they have produced other colours, white, orange, pink and red. The plants like plenty of winter sun and a rich limy mix to grow in, but will tolerate a certain amount of shade in the summer, when they are dormant.

In a wild area beyond the bottom of my garden the common gorse *Ulex europaeus* has spread over the years to make a flame of golden colour and it seems to flower at any time, but makes a particular splash in March. The double variety *Ulex europaeus fl. pl.* is more compact and originated in the west of England, its main flowering time being in February, though sometimes earlier. *Ulex gallii* and *Ulex nanus*, another native species, start flowering in the autumn and prostrate themselves over the headlands by the sea in a blaze of yellow. Any poor sandy bank that needs a spread of colour would benefit from the planting of these very much taken-for-granted plants, whose only snag is the protective spines that make them unsuitable for growing in a much used part of the garden. But the birds are grateful for the sharp thorns and make nests in the bushes, safe from most predators.

With similar yellow flowers, in colour only, are many of the tiny narcissus plants which will poke their heads through the soil if it's warm enough in February, but in a cold winter they will not be seen till early March. Some are so small they need a confined pocket in the rockery to look at their best; I think they are lost in a bed or border. *N. asturiensis* is only 3 in high with a frilled miniature golden trumpet, known as *minimus* and exactly the shape of the big trumpet daffodils coming later on in the spring. The next smallest is *N. bulbocodium tenuifolius* which is 5 in, 2 in shorter than the *N. bulbocodium conspicuus*, the well-known Hoop Petticoat, the shape of the corolla being very remindful of the old Victorian hoop petticoats swaying in the wind. There is a creamy-coloured variety from Morocco, *N. bulbocodium romieuxii*, in between the height of the previous two, which will flower much earlier, even at the beginning of the winter; and last a long time, braving the frost well. They are very dainty bulbs, with their grass-like foliage heightening this effect.

Another miniature daffodil, again about 6 in high, is *N. 'Tête-a-tête'*, a bright yellow, and *N. triandrus albus*, the so-called Angel's Tears with a white cup like a tear falling below reflexed spiralled petals; and a similar shape but with an even narrower corolla tube of chrome-yellow, with wings flattened away from it, is *N. cyclamineus*. All these, and many more of the species, can add their charm and scent to the other flowers in the rockery.

Leucojum has the lovely name of Snowflake, or white violet, and there are different varieties flowering in late spring, summer and autumn, but *L. vernum* will produce its flowers, like a pretty white lampshade tipped with green, in February or March and likes a moist position — perhaps where it can make drifts in light woodland — unlike the autumn kinds which prefer

Figure 5.6:
*Narcissus bulbocodium
conspicuus*

a dry sunny position. *L. vernum carpathicum* is a slightly later flowering Romanian form with yellow tips to the umbels, and two even larger flowers on each stem. There is a particularly attractive spring-flowering white one, *L. nicaeense* from the South of France only 4 in high, a third of the height of the *L. vernum*, and the small but tender pink flowered *L. roseum*, from Corsica, which blooms from August into September. So whatever the weather, you never need be without a snowflake flowering somewhere at some time.

To follow the little hardy *Cyclamen coum* which has been flowering sometimes as early as January, there is a really beautiful larger flowered kind from the Lebanon, *C. libanoticum*, with exquisitely scented blooms. They open in early March, a very pale pink, deepen to a rich salmon and then fade again as they age. There is a crimson marking at the base, said to resemble a bird in flight, and the rounded wavy-edged leaves, which develop before the flowers, have a greyish tinge to their green with the undersides bright purple. As with other cyclamen the corms like a good leafy soil and will grow under trees as long as the area is well-drained. They prefer a heavy lime content where they will establish after some years, but they do not flower the first year after planting. *C. libanoticum* is not easy to succeed with, but in warm areas of the country or a protected site in the garden, away from cold ground winds, it can be covered with dry leaves or bracken in winter or kept fairly snug under a rock ledge; then in spring after flowering it can be fed with a good mulch and a little bonemeal. It is often difficult to tell which way up to plant cyclamen tubers, but if in real doubt, plant them on their side and they will right themselves.

The Lenten Rose, *Helleborus orientalis*, has now been hybridised to produce a variety of colours, ranging from white, cream, pink, amaranth and red, the tints soft and shadowy. The leaves are large and handsome but the old ones need to be removed to keep the plant tidy. Then it makes a nice clump and blooms over many weeks, and in March will be joined by *H. viridis*, the smallest of the hellebores, known as Bear's-foot, and although a native of the Pyrenees, it is found wild elsewhere. The flowers are a purer green than *H. corsicus* with a faint but sweet scent. This species revels in lime and is one of the herbaceous group and so the plant dies right down in the summer and there is no foliage to be seen.

Of all the many kinds of primula there are, a treasure can always be found to fit into a nook in the rock garden, some requiring moist shady situations and others dry and sunny. My particular favourite is *P. winteri* (now known as *P. edgeworthii*), which is not descriptive of its habit of flowering from January through to March, because it refers, in fact, to the man who discovered it in the Himalayas. The pale lavender flowers have a central orange eye ringed by a zone of white and the leaves are toothed and covered when young with a curious white meal. This primula likes to be planted in the shade on its side, but in a well-drained soil. *P. × juliana* 'Wanda' is a deep claret colour and is a hybrid from the *P. juliae* from the

Figure 5.7:
Leucojum vernum 'Snowflake'

Caucasus, a shorter beautiful little plant packed with magenta flowers; they both give blooms of such rich and striking tones. A little taller is *P. garryarde*, a group of hybrid primroses of Irish origin with wrinkled green or bronzy leaves and heads of daintily frilled much larger flowers in several shades of white, pink and purple-violet. With a similar range of colour but a totally different stemmed flower-head is *P. denticulata*, with a 1 ft tall mop head of bloom before the leaves are fully grown. But these last two primulas don't always flower within the winter period. The season needs to be favourable to bring them on at the beginning of March, and of course a warm protected site helps too, be it sunny or shady to suit the needs of the particular type.

Saxifraga make up an enormous group of alpine plants for the rock garden. The largest number flower in spring and summer, but one or two very choice varieties will make cushions of flower, as their name indicates, brightening the early months of the year.

In one of the main five sections, *S. kabschia* (the Cushion Saxifrage), a hybrid *S. × burseriana*, has tight mats of silvery green and produces proportionately large flowers of either white or yellow on red stalks only 3 in high. A little earlier in March, *S. × apiculata* blooms make their appearance from rosettes of sharply pointed leaves grouped in clusters of three, of the palest curd yellow. This is a hardy little variety soon developing into a veritable cushion of bloom. But the first one flowering in the New Year is *S. kellereri*, the soft pink blooms appearing above the grey hump of leaves.

In this *kabschia* section the plants need a gritty soil, preferring a mixture of leaf-mould, sandy loam and limestone. They should be kept moist, but never soggy, at the roots, especially in summer when they will not like to be dried out by hot sun. A cranny between rocks or in crazy paving can make an ideal home for one of these delightful tussocks covered in their bright flowers.

Another plant — a bulb with an enormous range — is the crocus, to give blooms right through the winter. My favourite crocus I never planted at all, but it appeared one year growing near the fence, from the garden next door, and since then has gradually increased and seeded itself round the beds and the rock garden. *C. tomasinianus* has pale lavender long-necked flowers, the inner petals of which are a deeper mauve; and there are other richer colour forms, the best a deep purple, paler within, *C. tomasinianus* 'Whitewell Purple', a nice reversion in colour of the common one.

Also dotted all over the rockery, singly or in groups, the bright globes of the *C. aureus*, originally from Bulgaria, make an intense and one of the brightest orange-yellow splashes; such a good contrast to the rich violet of the Greek *C. sieberi*, of which there are various attractive forms. Unfortunately the birds go for the bright colour of the yellow crocus, but I do not try to protect these with black cotton now, having once done this and found a bird the next morning with its feet ensnared in the web of threads. I managed to save it, but have since decided that I can manage without the few flowers that they choose, for some unexplained reason, to peck at.

A very tiny little crocus that needs to be specially placed in the rockery as it would be lost in grass is *C. susianus* from Susa, in Iran. It has the beautiful name Cloth of Gold and is old gold in colour with velvety-brown markings on the outside. To complement this and an inch shorter is a small white crocus, *C. vernus albiflorus*, slim when closed but opening to a star with six pointed petals. *C. biflorus* from south-west Europe has larger flowers of the palest lavender feathered with purple, and there is a very charmingly-named form *C. biflorus* 'Weldenii Fairy' which is white with grey markings outside.

One of the finest forms from Greece and Asia Minor, *C. chrysanthus*, has a large number of colours in the range of yellow, white and purple, many of them named after birds; *C. chrysanthus* 'Snow Bunting' being white with a golden throat. Most of the crocus have some scent, *C. biflorus* and *C. chrysanthus*, I think, are particularly strong and evocative of the time of year.

The last flower is the humble sweet violet *V. odorata* which, although principally spring flowering from April to May, will often bloom freely during the winter months as well. It likes shady corners or banks under deciduous trees and prefers a heavy neutral soil, for it must never be allowed to dry out as the roots are shallow. There are five colours, apart from the colour of its name, these being white, pink, sulphur yellow and apricot. And there are single and double forms. They increase rapidly by runners to make a carpet of scent, the kidney-shaped leaves being as fragrant as the blooms.

These twenty weeks of winter, roughly ten in the old and ten in the new year, can be an exciting season in the garden and make the year flow with a continuous stream of flowering plants. Some of the pleasure comes, I find, from the discovery of a shrub or tiny bulb that will unfold its buds, however inclement the weather, in the darkest of days, and make the garden worth being in, or looking out on, from some vantage-point in the warmth of the house. A branch will always come into flower earlier and undamaged if cut for the safety and scenting of a room, but for me the real joy is to let it bloom naturally in the place you have chosen with such care for it. I can't think of anything else that can give such uncomplicated pleasure to see than a tree laden with blossom, or a miniature alpine opening a fresh bud, and throwing their perfume on the sharp air. And the process is on-going, for I am constantly discovering new plants, so there is always something to look forward to and to look after, and I believe the garden appreciates their presence too; for a neglected one is a sad sight.

There surely can't be many more rewarding occupations than to be a gardener.

Chapter 6

Tender Shrubs and Plants

In the previous chapters from November to March I have mentioned, occasionally, a tender variety of plant or a fragile species that will only grow in the most favourable conditions and climates of the country. But they will sometimes flourish in an otherwise unsuitable part of the world if the site is sheltered. When you think of the position of Scotland, for instance, which can be so cold and bleak and wind-driven, there are gardens on the west coast there, with a micro-climate influenced by the Gulf Stream (which also has similar effects on certain areas of the North American Atlantic shore-line, like the southern tip of Florida) where fantastic plants are to be found, and seen and enjoyed, too, by visitors should the garden be one of those open for public view. And there is the famous island of Tresco, off the coast of Cornwall, England, and another off the coast of southern Ireland, where tropical plants grow in abundance, additionally protected by a barrier of trees or strategically placed and well-grown hedges. And, of course, many of the great houses have gardens with especially sheltered positions.

Many years ago we feared that the land beyond our garden would be built on, and as we wanted seclusion, we planted a hedge of escallonia right along the bottom of our property. We first contacted a special research department, who were growing different varieties of this shrub, to try and find out which grew the fastest, and which ones stood up to fearful winds and made a good barrier. Although we originally envisaged it as a shield to make the garden private, this hedge has become a bonus we hadn't thought of at the time of planting. We were told the plants would reach 8 ft in four years, and in good areas of the hedge they did, though they took much longer to reach such a height where the hedge passed under trees already well-grown. But finally we had our wall of aromatic glossy evergreen leaves which, if pruned as the research station advised, flowered twice a year, becoming a mass of rich pink blooms; and it now made a wonderful protection for the wide border in front of it. So that plants, many of them tender and winter flowering, were not blasted by the prevailing westerly winds as they had been, and were allowed to bloom in peace.

In front of this protection, shrubs like the fleshy-leaved tender variety of veronica, *Hebe speciosa*, have prospered and come right through the winter, flowering on and off with their bright blue and also pink flowers. The barrier of the hedge and the slight overhang from tall deciduous trees above, give just the cover these particular hybrids need. Only in the very sudden cold and northerly wind of the new year in 1985, after weeks of mildness, were they affected, their leaves becoming shrivelled and brown. But when the damaged foliage is pruned away later on they should break from the base, for the well-formed root system should still be intact and although the stems above ground are temporarily diminished, the plants will grow very quickly to their former size of a 6 ft sq bush.

Though for over two weeks at the end of January and early February of 1985 it was very mild again, this early cold snap was very damaging, because the weeks before Christmas 1984 had been very mild too and so the plants were growing and the sap rising and the branches remained soft and very susceptible, not so much to the heavy snowfall as to the killing frosts we experienced for a few nights a little later, from brilliantly clear skies. Just as the snow had melted and the plants thought they'd made it, they were subjected to this fierce treatment with no snow blanket to protect them. To cap it all the bitter cold and snow returned in the second week of February — a proper seesaw of temperatures.

A ceanothus, *C. dentatus*, covering a wall of my garage looked very browned and will certainly be lost on the outside. I hope it will revive from the base and within the centre of the plant. But this is the first time in around ten years that this lovely blue climber has been so badly affected by the cold; normally the odd chill drying wind browns the edges of the foliage, but this is always renewed in the spring, when the burn can be snipped away. But the battering it had was very severe; still, I hope it will not prove lethal. If the worst does happen, I have a cutting of some years which has grown into a 10 in high plant, even though still in a pot, and I have this to replace it with, if necessary. But I suspect the main stem will have survived, protected as it is by the garage wall where it is 4 in across, and also by the outer branches and foliage which have been so damaged.

The escallonias at the bottom of the garden give sufficient shelter for the *Lavatera olbia* 'Rosea' bushes in the border — which form quite a hedge in themselves — to go on flowering, well into the beginning of the winter period; for the lack of wind and overhead canopy of tree branches encourages them to put out blooms until the very cold weeks of winter set in.

To find out whether the more tender plants can be grown in your area it is a good idea to look around at neighbouring gardens, and in the parks and public gardens, to see what they have; and even then you still have the fall-back of a sheltered site you can allocate to your plant to give it additional help through the difficult days. Here where I live it is very sunny but colder and frostier than a similar latitude 200-300 miles to the west, or gardens in Florida or on the California coast. We have palm trees tucked away in sunken or sheltered gardens — I have two I have grown in mine — but they are not grown on the sea-front and in exposed positions, as they are in more favourable areas, where the climate approaches that of the Mediterranean. Similarly, I always remember seeing free-standing trees of mimosa, *Acacia dealbata*, growing as large as oaks in a milder district, but here they must have the protection of a southern house wall. But, nevertheless, they do grow roof-high despite the quite considerable difference in climate between the two areas. So for tender plants, obviously the site really is the main consideration.

There are more than half-a-dozen tender varieties of jasmine listed in catalogues, most of them sweetly scented and flowering during late spring or summer. But there are two that are winter flowering, the one I grow *J. mesnyi* the Primrose Jasmine, introduced here from China, which is evergreen and has much larger and brighter flowers than the ordinary winter *J. nudiflorum*. From Madeira there comes another tender summer- and winter-blooming jasmine, *J. azoricum*, which must be grown in the greenhouse unless a really warm spot can be found for this rather special evergreen with its heavily scented white flowers, deep pink in bud. I shall start mine, when I can get it, in the greenhouse and then gradually acclimatise it and plant it in a well protected corner, covering it in cold weather with straw, or fronds of plants, or even plastic sheeting stretched across it so that the wall will give it just the warmth it needs. I have seen large 20 ft high geranium plants covered in this way in warmer parts and surviving out-of-doors under the added cover of a porch, but still in the open air, which is the kind of success I aim for.

Another attractive climber, from the other side of the world, in Chile, is *Eccremocarpus scaber* which is so easy to grow and climbs very rapidly. It sets such large bags of seed that if the main plants do succumb, one can easily produce more to take their place. But though the upper tendrils get damaged in winter, unless there have been very prolonged cold stretches, shoots will break from the base next year. The bright orange clustered flowers, like narrow bells, and the soft-green delicate foliage makes this an entrancing plant to grow. Because of the prolific seeding it can be treated and grown very successfully as an annual, but I like to wrap it up in felt and plastic above ground and cover the base with a pile of compost, and bring the original plant through the winter if I can. This climber is grown very satisfactorily 400 miles north of me and has survived the ravages of a severe winter there, flowering against a wall well into November, if the seed-bags are removed regularly; which means it is a real contender for one of the early winter flowerers in various temperate zones.

An intriguing plant from Australia with similar shaped flowers, but of a soft greenish-yellow, white and pink and scarlet, is the shrub correa. The leaves are oval and green, a little like those of a camellia, but with grey undersides, and totally unlike the delicate light-green sprays of the eccremocarpus. These little plants are rarely seen in gardens, but would be worth trying as their small size means they can be more easily protected. I would like to try *C. pulchella*, which has almond-pink flowers all winter.

Despite their relegation to the greenhouse in the early part of the century, the camellia plants are perfectly hardy and are always grown in the open nowadays. But the variety must be chosen with care, and some species like *C. sasanqua* are not so hardy as the *C. japonica* in all its varieties, though it blooms in early winter and has the great advantage of scented flowers, so it is one of my favourites. I grow the white *C. sasanqua* 'Narumi-gata' and the blood-red *C. sasanqua* 'Crimson King', both with single blooms. In cooler, more northerly, parts of the country where the daylight is shorter, *C. × williamsii* hybrids seem to fare better even than the *C. japonica*. For not only must the plant survive, but unless the conditions are right it will not flower. So I move a plant that does not seem happy. However, a camellia I grew from a leaf someone gave me, when first planted against a northern wall dropped its flower-buds every year and I meant to move it but didn't get round to it; and suddenly it began holding its flowers and is now 4 ft sq and covers itself in double pink blooms every spring. Possibly it was too dry against the wall until the roots had grown sufficiently to reach down for adequate moisture and nourishment. Or perhaps there was too much lime in the upper soil initially. At any rate I am very pleased with my plant now, remembering it came from a leaf of a 50 ft high tree, standing in a garden near me, and which it is amazing to think Queen Victoria may have seen growing as a small shrub when she stayed nearby.

Another case of picking your varieties is with the snowflakes, *Leucojum*, a relation of the snowdrop, where the hardier species flower in the spring, such as *L. vernum*; but the autumn-flowering *L. autumnale* needs protection from a cold winter so that its delicate pink-flushed white bells will not be broken down by sharp winds catching its fine 6 in stems. Another even more tender snowflake, barely 4 in high with the palest of pink flowers in early autumn, *L. roseum*, needs even more shelter as it comes from the island of Corsica in the Mediterranean. Save in very favourable mild parts of the country, I think this little bulb would be safer in a pot, so that it can be carried under cover during a severe turn in the weather.

A very tender clematis which flowers from December onwards is *C. napaulensis*, also known as *C. forrestii*. The cream-coloured blooms have striking mauve stamens inside the cups of flower, but the plant is only semi-evergreen, needing a great deal of shelter to enable it to hold on to its leaves.

With many plants the question of keeping or losing the leaves does depend on the amount of protection they receive — that is, apart from the general replacement and renewal constantly recurring in the evergreen species. Petunias, for instance, are summer-flowering annuals in this country, but if brought into a greenhouse they can be kept going and flowering in a pot, and will survive to be planted out next summer. I remember the surprise I felt once when visiting a friend's garden in the South of France to see large bushes of petunias, which the owner pruned and treated as permanent shrubs. I suppose a very atypical winter frost there might do for them, but from then on I realised that any of the annuals we grow here, if treated kindly, would behave in the same way.

Like the correa plants, the grevillea shrubs also come from Australia and Tasmania, and the 1 ft high G. *alpina* which flowers all the year round, has curious spider-like cream and red flowers set on rosemary type foliage. There are two other kinds, G. *thyrsoides* and G. *rosmarinifolia* which flower in winter too, from January to August, not all the year, but as they grow to 5 or 6 ft they are terribly vulnerable, and need the very warmest areas and a totally sheltered site. But I grow G. *alpina* in my rockery, tucked between stones in a peaty compost, as all these plants like a lime-free soil. When the cold arrives I build a little screen round it, which I can put a lid on in heavy frost, and in that way it will survive out of doors, here. But it is in its element in climates such as California can provide. Because of its continuous flowering and bright blooms and foliage it is a special love of mine, and I like trying to get it to succeed in my garden.

Lardizabala biternata is an evergreen climber not often seen or written about but it runs up to 25 ft or more with bright green leathery leaves and a profusion of drooping sprays of purple and white flowers throughout the winter months. It does need a warm sheltered wall in the milder parts of the country and will grow very attractively over an arch. The flowers are followed by elongated purple fruits which are edible. It likes a well-drained soil with leaf-mould and peat added and only needs pruning in spring when the growths are getting too crowded.

The sharp-yellow pea flowers of *Coronilla glauca*, which just keep on and on blooming and crowding the bush without cease in a sheltered sunny site, stand up to the cold in my garden remarkably well for many months of the year, though this is far from its home in southern Europe. To the north, if no really protected place can be found, it will make a delightful pot plant or thrive in and scent a glasshouse, the acid-yellow flowers so bright against the sea-green bloom of the foliage.

A shrub just over a foot high which bears intense blue flowers and has leaves a little like the grevilleas and certainly very like a rosemary, is called *Lithospermum rosmarinifolium*. This is a tender winter-flowering variety from southern Italy so it needs protection in our winter and most of all a dry neutral soil. Damp and cold will surely kill it. But in a favoured corner it develops hard woody stems and from among the slim dark-green leaves bloom the large gentian-like flowers during January and February. I think this is a very choice shrub to have and worth the extra care needed to preserve it.

A flower of a much paler blue but with enormous blooms like a lilac is the *Ceanothus arboreus* 'Trewithen Blue'. This is the tree form of the many varieties of Californian Lilacs which are usually grown as bushes or climbers. The leaves are very large and this variety came originally from a garden famous for its tender plants, in a very mild part of the country. Again it seems happiest kept fairly dry on a poor stony soil and suffers when the conditions are cold and wet. It grows very fast, once away to a good start, and my three-year-old tree is already 12 ft high, and an older tree I know of stands without any protection, flowering all the year round, summer and winter, apparently able to stand up to any snow or cold wind that's blowing. But it would certainly want and appreciate the shelter of a wall in a colder area.

All the sunny warmth possible is needed for a dear little corm named *Romulea bulbocodium* to open its flowers in late winter, with yellow-centred mauve blooms among leaves as fine as grass. In colder areas, it can be grown in the greenhouse in flat pots with a layer of grit on the surface to keep the very short-stalked flowers free of the soil.

Someone once brought me a pot containing a plant I didn't know, for it was a variety of ranunculus from North Africa, *R. calandrinioides*. The flowers were like a buttercup but a clear rose-pink with a tiny mop of deep-yellow stamens, and the leaves were slim and as delicate as the flower. It is often grown under glass in unfavourable areas, but as it blooms in February to March it is nice to have outdoors in a sheltered place to catch the late winter sun, and join the other plants a few inches high appearing in the rockery at this time.

A variety of the small outdoor cyclamens, but with much larger flowers, which are also sweetly scented, is *C. libanoticum*. It does not like cold winds but on a sloping site away from this hazard will gradually establish itself and produce pale pink flowers which deepen in colour as they age, and they have a crimson mark at the base which is very impressive. The tuber grows, in time, very large and circular and becomes corky. In the same way as the previous plants, if enough protection cannot be found, this cyclamen will enjoy the extra warmth an alpine house can give.

Primula allionii is a rock-dwelling primula and a slightly tender one out of the huge number and variety that flower at all times of the year. It blooms in March and comes from the limestone reaches of the Alps, which tower over France and Italy. It has sticky grey-green leaves and makes a 2 in dome over which the rose-pink flowers cluster with their yellow and white centres. It must have very good drainage and a decent amount of sun to do well, and likes a stony mixture to remind it of its mountainous homeland, where it often grows wedged between rocks.

Saxifraga grisebachii belongs to the *Engleria* section of this very diverse group of plants. It flowers from January to March forming flat humps of spoon-shaped leaves, silvery-green but crimson at the base. A 6 in stem comes from the centre of the rosette with a purple flower and also occasional reddish bracts up the stem. A very striking and unusual saxifrage, there being an even more notable form, *S. grisebachii* 'Wisley Variety' with brighter and larger blooms. They like a gritty soil, ideally a mixture of limestone, leaf-mould and light sandy loam, whether they are planted in a favoured spot in the rockery or displayed on trays within the protection of an alpine house. Outside they need to be kept moist — though not wet — in summer, if not shaded from the high sun.

Sheltered gardens provide the ideal conditions for many tender trees and shrubs, and there can be grown a mimosa which flowers nearly all the year round. *Acacia rhetinoides* is very useful as, of all the mimosas, most of which originated in Australia, it is most tolerant of lime in the ground where it is planted. The sprays of pretty yellow flowers hang from branches of long slim leaves, not unlike the *A. longifolia* or Sydney Golden Wattle which I grow in my garden near the cost, also tolerant of some lime.

I have come to the conclusion after many years of trying to grow plants of a more fragile disposition than the climate in my garden would normally allow, that one of the most important considerations when assessing the chances of my succeeding with them, is something now referred to as the wind chill factor. A cool wet wind is fine, bitter cold in a still atmosphere can be countered by boxed or wrapped protection, but when a freezing cold drying wind is blowing strongly, it whips up the snow, tears off the protective covering and lowers the temperature of the plant, to say nothing of the individual, to a previously unrealised degree. So this is the great danger to watch out for when trying to preserve your tender plants. An example of the difference the wind makes is that in a temperature of say 23°F and a biting easterly gale, these combine to produce the equivalent temperature of −58°F on a still sunny day. A fearful combination. No wonder it can kill man or beast, in addition to the poor plants — and those particular ones so totally unused and unprepared to cope with such cold.

However, if the danger is recognised and allowed for, and these tender specialities found the most sheltered positions you have, out of range of the deadly combination, then, except in the very worst and prolonged of winters, they will survive and reward you with their beautiful flowers.

Another very important factor when trying to grow tender plants is that they should always be planted in a well-drained pocket, the soil broken up by rubble or grit. Very often the plants have to stand 20° or more of frost in their native habitat, yet half that temperature with soggy conditions will finish them off in this country. And it is a great help to plant them in the spring, so that they have the summer to put down their roots and get established before they face their first winter. And this, if safely got through, will give them a much better chance of surviving future years. Should the first summer be very dry, mulching and overhead spraying will help them while they are settling in.

================Chapter 7================

Shrubs and Plants for Sunny Spots and Walls

The sun plays such an important part in the growth of all living things: but several plants can survive in areas where very little reaches them; while for others it is essential for the ripening of their wood to set the flowers; and even with some plants the flowers do not open unless the sun is shining directly upon them. So it is vital to find out just how much it is known is needed for the particular shrub or bulb you are planting. Then it can produce its maximum effect and so renew itself and increase in size by growing well.

Walls offer a very desirable site for plants in the garden. Not only do they give an excellent background and set off whatever is being grown — whether it is a tree, a climber, a shrub or the smallest bulb or herbaceous plant — but the protection they obviously give means an increased temperature, so that on a warm sunny wall sub-tropical and other delicate specimens can be grown with confidence. In large cities the effect of so many buildings can increase the local climate by around 10° and certainly I have noticed that even though I live 60 miles south of a major city, the plants there all flower about a month before anything in my garden; all those walls build up the temperature and therefore the natural protection, so altering the temperature zone in which it is situated.

This is even more important in winter when they will protect from the cold winds and it is surprising how many spots can be found to tuck away some favoured plant. And a sunny place is also appreciated by certain shrubs and bulbs which are quite hardy, but need a good baking to ripen the plant or the wood of the stems, in order to produce fine flowers later on.

A good example of a tough plant that likes this sun to ripen the wood is the Winter Sweet, *Chimonanthus praecox (fragrans)*. The flowers are not delicate and papery but thick and wax-like and so protected from, and suffer happily, all the nasty weather that may be thrown at them. The plant is also easy as to the type of soil it is planted in, even liking chalk, so it should be on your short list if you happen to be making a garden on such land. I had a well-grown shrub, about 4 ft high, just appearing above the window against my south wall and so the yellow flowers, with their rich maroon inner petals, were visible, and remained undamaged, even in a heavy rain-storm. Unfortunately I lost this plant, due to over-enthusiastic help from my son-in-law who pruned it down to the ground, and it promptly died! This is not a plant that likes much pruning and against a wall can be spread out to indulge itself in the sun's warmth so the branches will ripen well and produce flowers that much earlier in its life. And when they do bloom that heavy scent in winter is unforgettable.

By experimenting with clumps of the *Iris unguicularis (stylosa)* in different parts of my garden I have found that the place where they give most flowers is on a northerly wall which gets no sun at all in winter, but in summer the arc of the sun swings round in the afternoon to bake this particular raised bed of poor hard soil, which is backed by a low brick wall, and the roots really get very cooked during the high summer siesta times. Then when you turn this cold corner in winter, there are the masses of flowers — a marvellous dividend.

Profiting from this experience, I planted beside the steps in the rockery a new variety to me, from the Black Sea, *I. lazica*, which has slightly smaller but much deeper mauve flowers; similarly, I put another one in a place where no sun reaches it in the winter, but a corner baked in summer. And, in the first year, it has produced its vivid stubby blooms, opening even more effectively than usual against a thick white contrast of snow. Here again, sun at the right time and in the right place has produced good results.

My two favourite winter flowers are from the shrubs of the winter honeysuckle *Lonicera fragrantissima* and the *Coronilla glauca*, which grow and bloom side by side on the southern front of the house. The latter is tender, but against a sunny warm wall will come through quite severe winters here. The honeysuckle produces its scented flowers all winter, the plant's wood benefiting from the ripening qualities of the sun, whenever it shines, in summer or winter. The coronilla, which is also very sweetly scented, but evergreen, with its shiny foliage is a good contrast to the bare branches of the deciduous lonicera nearby. And these combinations make up the texture of the garden, so that everything a tree or shrub or small plant or bulb possesses — be it bare outline clothed in flowers; rich green foliage with blooms among it; small plant a mass of leaves with flowers appearing out of them; or others where the flower comes clean out of the earth before the leaves arrive — these must all be taken into account and visualised, and then the balance of the garden will be right. I have my summer-flowering evergreen cistus plants strategically placed everywhere in the garden, not only for their summer blooming, but to make a good backdrop, especially to the deciduous winter-flowering plants and bulbs.

Then, behind an evergreen shrub, a clematis will grow very happily on a sunny wall, for it likes its roots to be cool, as they are hidden behind the bush and yet it grows into the sun to flower against the warmth of the wall. A little unlike most clematis, the winter-flowering *C. cirrhosa* types do well also on a shaded colder wall, despite their place of origin in the more southern Mediterranean regions. Though I don't grow mine in this position. I feel the delicate evergreen foliage needs protection from the prevailing westerly winds here, which would catch the climber if I had planted it anywhere but in a sheltered southern corner. But by March it was still flowering, untouched by the various fierce spells that winter had produced.

The abelias are a group of shrubs that love the sun. They rarely exceed 6 ft in height, some evergreen and others deciduous, this often depending on the severity of the winter and their position in the garden. I have *A. schumannii* planted between stones in the rockery in a very sunny position, and I trim it well to keep the long shoots it throws out within bounds of the other plants around it, and to make a nicely-shaped shrub which flowers in July and goes on well into November, the lush green leaves turning bronze so that there is a three-tone effect on this very delicate bush and it holds its leaves till hard frost comes. My other taller-growing *A. grandiflora* I planted against a very sunny warm fence and this I let keep its long shoots, to spread and decorate the grey oak of the protecting fence, and except in the most bitter of winters, it will remain covered in its darker-green leaves.

Two sun-loving lily bulbs, set between the abelia and the wall of the house and growing in a light sandy mixture, are surrounded by protective boulders, which reflect heat on to the plants and encourage them to throw up their strong stems in the late autumn, as they are both half-hardy. One is *Nerine bowdenii*, and the other, twice as tall, is *Amaryllis belladonna*. They make a lovely pair, the first a spidery flower, the second with thick rich petals, a marked contrast to each other and the comparatively minute bells of the abelia, all felicitously growing and flowering within a few feet of each other. I feel they make a skilful grouping and complement each other, but I have to admit the planting was slightly more random than it appears now!

In this same area of the garden I have grown and lost and shall try again with the honey-scented buddleia from South Africa, *B. auriculata*. In winter I could open the windows on a sunny day and the creamy flowers, though only 2 in long and smaller than the common summer-flowering buddleias, would nevertheless give off a much stronger scent than the large lilac-shaped *B. davidii* species. The general appearance of the shrub is felty white, as the evergreen leaves are a very pale almond-green with clothy-white undersides. The tube-like flowers are composed of tiny individual little trumpets with a touch of yellow inside.

A balcony, even in an upper apartment, or the first-floor windows of a house, should always be catered for. Of course the simplest idea would seem to be to have pots and window-boxes on a balcony, but this means you have condemned yourself to a lifetime of watering. A tree or climber can be planted directly into the soil, in a bed round the base of the building, and grown up the walls to be seen and smelled on the balcony or out of the window. There are a great number of climbers which will do this very rapidly; and a rose, for instance, will cover the side of a house in time and will go on flowering into winter, especially if it can be trained on to the added protection of the balcony and is regularly dead-headed. Though I can think of one occasion when this method proved disastrous. A friend with an upper apartment had always enjoyed the beautiful pink apple-scented wichuraiana rose 'François Juranville' clambering round her balcony. One day she returned to find that the owner of the apartment below, outside which the rose was planted, had pruned it to the ground, and she was left scent-less and rose-less after years of pleasure.

On a warm wall, in sun — though it will take some shade as long as the position is sheltered — the evergreen climber *Lardizabala biternata*, a native of Chile, will grow fairly rapidly to reach up to 30 ft and the bright green foliage covers the wall all summer, when a clematis could be planted to climb up and flower among its twining stems. Then all winter the hanging purple and white flowers of the lardizabala would display their striking blooms.

What a sight the heaths make flowering along a bank in the winter sunshine. And the varieties that bloom during the cold months are very easy to grow as they do not mind lime in the soil. Whether it is the dwarf mounds of *Erica carnea* or the taller-growing *E. darleyensis* or *E. mediterranea*, they become very compact if the spent flowers are regularly clipped to shape after blooming, so that they are useful as ground cover in pockets of the rockery or for filling a whole bed to make an island of continuous and solid colour. If the whole area is planted with selected varieties which give flower each and every month of the year, the clumps which are not flowering at that moment form a dense moss-green mass beside those in bloom. Greater contrast can be had when the varieties with bronze-gold or yellow foliage are mixed among the greens.

Another elegant plant to grow in drifts is the Irish Heath, *Daboecia cantabrica*, related to the ericas. It has shades of magenta and white flowers from mid-summer into early winter, the blooms being larger in long sprays. But this genus hates lime.

A shrub or small tree from California, *Arctostaphylos manzanita*, which will not tolerate any lime or chalk in the soil, being related to the other acid-loving group of ericas and also allied to the rhododendrons, likes plenty of sun to produce its rather heath-like flowers, white pitchers tinged with pink among the thick oval leaves and reddish peeling bark. A very striking sight against a white wall, although it is not a tender shrub, but the wall would reflect the sun to encourage the plant to do well and so flower profusely, and earlier in the year.

The Loquat, *Eriobotrya japonica*, grows to tree size in warmer climates and produces edible fruits, but in England it is usually grown as a shrub against a sunny wall; for the thick and indented, crinkly leaves, sometimes 1 ft long, need protection. The scented creamy flowers open, on and off, during the winter, in the years when there has been a really hot summer. But there is a very fine tree-size specimen to be seen topping a protective wall not far from me and it makes a truly dramatic sight.

The Brooms, cytisus and genista, and the Spanish Broom, *Spartium junceum*, which are all closely related, like a sunny position and they can vary from dwarf prostrate forms to tree-size bushes. Most of them have yellow pea-shaped flowers. Two which flower in the autumn and very often go into winter and continue flowering spasmodically when the weather's mild, are *Genista tinctoria* — the dwarf 'Plena' and 'Royal Gold' being very attractive for the rockery, and *Cytisus nigricans* with long arches of flower late in the year. I have an unnamed variety which seeds itself everywhere and grows very tall and leggy if left untrimmed. Yet sheared to a nice round head two or three times a year it can be kept within bounds, and is quite tough, remaining evergreen through a very cold winter and throwing out the odd chrome-bright flower.

The three heights and shapes of *Prunus subhirtella* 'Autumnalis' which produce such delicate pink-washed white flowers every mild spell in the winter, all of them — the 30 ft tree on a sloping bank, the 20 ft high standard topping the terrace wall, and the 10 ft half-standard framing the bay window — look twice as effective when the sun is out, as they have all been positioned so that they do get the maximum amount available at all times of the year. This, again, helps them to set the flowers which string the slender arching branches in winter. They all give a choice of views: if I look up from under the tree, the flowers are framed against the blue sky; if I glance out of an upstairs window, the standard has a background of green grass below the darker green of a fir tree; or when I am on the drive, the pale pink blooms of the half-standard are pictured against the stark white walls of the house. So these three trees form the backdrop of my winter garden.

Chapter 8

Shrubs and Plants for Shady Spots and Walls

How fortunate it is that some plants will grow in shade, for however carefully a garden is sited — even those specially designed in conjunction with a house to use the natural light and warmth of the sun and protect from wind — there are inevitably several spots which will fall in shade and where a flower appearing there will delight the eye and in winter lessen the gloom of the darkened area; somewhere that, at the height of summer, may be appreciated as a place to get out of the heat and glare of the day.

All the sarcococcas will grow in dense shade and several attain quite a reasonable size, for what is initially a very small neat shrub. There are four or five different species, each with distinctively-shaped leaves but the bunches of white flowers from the leaf axils are particularly sweetly scented in *S. humilis* and *S. confusa* and *S. hookeriana digyna*, but not in *S. saligna*, so it is important to get the right one.

The rather rare *Daphne blagayana* prefers to be growing in half-shade where it can spread its horizontal branches along near the ground. In a shady corner of the rockery, even under deciduous shrubs, it can scramble among the stones and benefits from limestone soil and leaf-mould. *D. laureola* is another variety that also likes partial shade.

A branch of the heathers and closely related to the ericas is the ling or *Calluna* (*Erica vulgaris*). It grows over the hills in Scotland and in the west of England, the common heath of the moorlands. My favourite one, which will flower into the early winter, is *C. vulgaris* 'H.E. Beale' with very long sprays of soft pink flowers, and these lings are taller than the ordinary ericas, being around 2 ft on average. They will thrive under the shade of trees in a woodland setting, making excellent ground cover.

Another plant that likes a woodland setting is the eucryphia tree. My evergreen hybrid *E. × intermedia* seems well settled amongst the protection of a rowan and a philadelphus tree, which shade it nicely from the heavy summer sun. And yet as it comes into flower they will soon lose their leaves, giving the eucryphia more light to carry on blooming, from August right up to Christmas in a reasonable year. The white flower-cups, with their purple anthers, stand out very clearly in the shade and against the dark background of the rich green polished leaves. Then in the spring when the rowan and philadelphus come into pale green leaf and flower, the dark columnar eucryphia makes a nice foil between the two.

There are roses that will grow well on a north wall, like the one I have on a north-east facing pergola, the rambler (wichuraiana) R. 'Alberic Barbier'. This makes a lovely mass of shiny, often evergreen, leaves with clusters of white flowers, cream in the bud, to cover and give a marvellous effect to what otherwise can be a very uninviting area of a house or garden. But the (Bourbon) R. 'Zephirine Drouhin' has two greater assets, it is thornless and its deep pink flowers are heavily scented; yet this rose is particularly happy on a north wall. For one of the most delightful gardens to have is an old one of ancient walls, where plants can be grown on the sunny or shady areas away from damaging wind and with the protection the walls give from frosts. And if the rose is kept well dead-headed then the odd bloom will open against the wall far into winter.

The Christmas Roses or hellebores like some sun and some shade, but one variety H. foetidus will thrive in a place with really bad light and put out its green bunches of flowers, which remain for weeks and turn red round the rims. I thought there was a limit, though, to what a plant can stand, and in a recent bitter cutting wind their apparently tough 2 ft stems were bent and frozen to the ground. But as the temperature rose again they miraculously righted themselves. For in the moderate conditions of a normal winter the plant is a real asset for a shady spot and easy to grow, increasing rapidly.

North walls should also be utilised to the fullest extent with shade-loving plants for the shelter they offer from wind which does such damage to plant leaves, particularly the fragile papery-thin types which give no protection to the framework, whereas the thicker and larger the leaf the tougher it is and the more shade it will stand, because it can take in more light through the large leaves.

One of the largest group of plants which really enjoy shady positions in the garden are the cydonias. I have various plants growing in the total shadow of a wall or of the house, in terrible soil under the stones of the terrace. Yet they seem to 'enjoy bad health' as the Victorian ladies were reputed to do and the adverse conditions apparently make no difference to this versatile chaenomeles with all its lovely choice of flower colour from pure white C. speciosa 'Nivalis' through pink and orange to the deepest double blood-red, C. speciosa 'Simonii', which I have mentioned before as being my favourite one.

Camellia japonica unlike C. sasanqua will tolerate quite a lot of shade and several of these camellias are upright in form and tall-growing and are an ideal plant for a north wall, whereas varieties like C. japonica 'Lady

Clare' and C. *japonica* 'Miss Universe' are neat and make a low compact shrub, spreading outwards but not often exceeding 2-3 ft in height. Should the space you have available be very restricted, the best two for planting which grow to a good height but not much across are the *williamsii* hybrids C. × 'E.G. Waterhouse' and C. × 'Anticipation', both ideal for a small garden. But I think camellias do look particularly fine grown against a solid background, and the long growths of certain hybrids can be trained close to walls, in the same way as a peach tree, and tied neatly around any windows. There is a lovely white formal double named C. *japonica* 'Mathotiana Alba', which will especially appreciate the protection a wall gives, and a salmon-pink flower, C. *japonica* 'Drama Girl' and two varying shades of pink, the Jury hybrid C. × 'Elegant Beauty' and C. *saluenensis* × *reticulata* 'Francie L'. All these four are ideal for providing bleak walls with a wonderful decoration in late winter.

Viburnum foetens very much enjoys a shady position unlike some of the other viburnums. *V. tinus*, for instance, revels in sunshine having come from the Mediterranean region. But *V. foetens* comes from Korea and the Himalayas and with its lax habit it needs half-woodland or a shady wall to prevent its large leaves from being beaten about in wind, and some overhead or wall cover will protect the flowers from being frosted.

The delicate ferny leaves of the tree *Azara microphylla* appreciate a position against a north wall, too, where the pungent vanilla scent from its yellow stamens are not blown away and dispersed by winter wind and cold.

So I like to think of each wall as having a particular use and purpose for the plant to benefit from, and for the gardener to enjoy to the full. And as one climber with evergreen heavy foliage will cover up the spare dry sticks that the clematis leaves in its wake, two evergreens each side of a tender shrub will give more protection than anything I can do for it, when the weather turns sharp.

Ground cover in the garden can be a complete cover up, like the heathers make in time and other plants develop, such as the invasive vincas and hypericum (St John's Wort), which are both difficult to control and keep within bounds. But the best cover is not a total one, but far more attractive, if requiring a bit more weeding. Bulbs such as muscari and scilla and snowdrop (galanthus) and snowflake (leucojum) are ideal. And all the wide choice from the narcissus family, from the minutest baby to the elegant tall-growing giants. Drifts look marvellous planted under deciduous trees, in mown grass or that kept roughly scythed as a 'natural' garden to encourage insects and butterflies; giving a small conservation area of your own. Cyclamen are so effective planted in this way, too, and all the primulas in their range of colours, not forgetting the plant that never fails to appear, the common primrose, *P. vulgaris*.

Another interesting way of growing small plants as ground cover under the shade of deciduous trees is to make a raised circular bed round the trunk of a tree, a method used, I believe, by the Moguls, to sit among the flowers out of the heat of the day. This is enclosed in a foot high wall of bricks; and of course, any special mixture of soil can be used in the bed, depending on what is to be grown. My neighbour has two silver birch trees done in this way, and I can see the multi-coloured flowers grouped round the pearly barks, above the circle of bricks, red against the green grass. So I have a delightful and unusual view, without having had to do the preparation!

And in the right soil, gritty, peaty and moist, a mass of *Gentiana sino-ornata* can be stunning. I have seen this done in light woodland, so the spreading stems form a mat of rosettes and when the flowers come there is a solid sea of intense blue glowing in the partial shade. The really important point I try to remember when growing any of the gentians, in whatever type of soil they require, is that they must be very firmly planted or they die on you! The spring-flowering G. *acaulis* needs a moderately heavy loam, and there are half-a-dozen summer flowering varieties that like a neutral soil and three that prefer an acid one, but G. *sino-ornata* is the one to grow for winter, as it flowers from September well into November, but it must have its lime-free soil.

The rockery perennial *Hepatica nobilis*, which is allied to the anemone family, looks very good in grass under trees, and the daisy-like flowers have a wide range from white and blue to pink and red. They increase from seeding themselves and make nice groups in shady corners of the rockery or down a grassy north-facing bank. And they are no trouble to grow at all.

I once saw a very attractive and clever way to plant the small *Iris reticulata*. On a turf-smooth incline, with a light canopy of trees overhead, the flowers were ranged like troops with their different colours in double lines, so that it was possible to see by comparison which variation in shade and marking was the one which would fit best into the overall colour scheme in another garden.

How much more satisfactory it is to see any plant in flower. Somehow the description on the page only approximates to the living thing and never comes up to the real beauty of the different textures involved, the felty or satiny surface of a petal, the gloss or hairiness of a leaf and the smoothness or flaking peel of a bark — though I am only concerned with flowers in this book, the others being mere adjuncts, and to my mind often admired quite out of proportion to the value which the flower and its scent can give.

Most of the viola family — the small-flowered kinds, the pansies and the true violets themselves — will all tolerate a shady position to light up a dull corner. I have some in low pots so that I can carry them around and place them wherever there is a blank part of the garden at that moment. For even with careful scheming and planting to have flowers in all parts of the garden at all times of the year — so important in winter — the weather will defeat your planning by being too mild or too cold and so advancing or holding back the time the flowers are supposed to bloom. This ruins the succession arrangement; but gardening is always a surprise and whatever one does to tame it, every year is different and defies all forecasts, especially in this country, where we are subject to so many variations in our weather, making the climate totally unpredictable. But just as soon as you feel the worst has happened, along comes another patch of glorious balm to confound you totally, and the experts too! So, particularly in winter, although other countries have their problems too, and also their own rewards, I find ours is a most stimulating country in which to garden.

Chapter 9

One Hundred Principal Plants for the Winter Flower Garden

Key
1. Name of plant — Genus, and species or variety.
   (Where 'various' under plant name, greater details can be found in text — see chapter numbers in column 15.)
2. Place of origin.
3. Type: a = Tree, b = Shrub, c = Climber, d = Herbaceous plants, alpines and herbs, e = Bulbs, tubers, corms and rhizomes.
4. Evergreen, Deciduous, Herbaceous or Perennial.
5. Maximum height of plant.
6. Maximum spread of plant.
7. Colour of flower.
8. Flowering time (months 1-12).
9. When to plant (months 1-12).
10. Soil: A = acid, B = neutral, C = alkaline, D = well-drained.
11. Position: S = sun, Sh = shade, T = Tender, needing shelter.
12. Pruning: x = hard, y = shaping and removal of dead wood, z = very little or none.
13. Propagation: Sd = seed, Ctg = cuttings, Lyg = layering, Div = division, Gr = grafting (months 1-12).
14. Hardiness: Zone 5 = −10° to −20°F, Zone 6 = 0° to −10°F, Zone 7 = 10° to 0°F, Zone 8 = 20° to 10°F.
15. Mentioned in Chapters: N = November, D = December, J = January, F = February, M = March, T = Tender, S = Sun, Sh = Shade.
16. Scent: 1 = strong, 2 = good, 3 = faint, 4 = none.

1	2	3	4	5	6	7	8	9	10	11	12	13	14	15	16
Abelia															
grandiflora	Unknown	b	E	6ft	3ft sq	white/pink	7-11	4	B	S/T	y	Ctg 7	Z 6/7	N/S	3
schumannii	China	b	D	3ft	2ft sq	pink	7-11	4	B	S/T	y	Ctg 7	Z 6/7	N/S	3
Abeliophyllum															
distichum	Korea	b	D	6ft	5ft sq	white	2	10-12	B	S	x/y	Ctg 7	Z6	F	2
Abutilon															
megapotamicum	Brazil	b	D	3ft	3ft sq	red & yellow	6-11	4	B	S/T	y	Ctg 7	Z 6/7	N/T	4
Acacia															
dealbata	Australia	a	E	12-20ft	8ft sq	yellow	2	4	B	S/T	y	Sd 4	Z 6/7	NJ/T	1
longifolia	Australia	a	E	12-20ft	8ft sq	yellow	7-1	4	B	S/T	y	or	Z 6/7	NJ	1
rhetinoides	Australia	a	E	10ft	6ft sq	yellow	6-11	4	B/C	S/T	y	Ctg 9	Z 6/7	T	1
Adonis															
various	Europe & Asia	d	H	6-12 in	9 in. sq	yellow & others	3	11	C	S	—	Div 9 or Sd 2	Z 5/6	M	4
Amaryllis															
belladonna	S. Africa	e	H	3ft	1ft sq	pink	9-11	6	A/B	S/T	—	Sd 3	Z7	N/S	4
Anemone															
blanda	Europe	e	H	4 in	12 in. sq	various	3	10	B	½Sh	—	Sd 7 or Div 7	Z6	M	4
coronaria	Mediterranean	e	H	8 in	4 in sq	various	3	9	B/D	S	—	Div 7	Z6	M	4
vernalis	Europe	d	E	4 in	9 in sq	white	3	8	C/D	S	—	Sd 7	Z 5/6	M	4
fulgens	Greece	e	P	9-12 in	4 in sq	scarlet	3	8-10	B/D	S/½Sh	—	Div 7 or Sd 8	Z7	M	4
Arbutus															
unedo	Mediterranean & Eire	a	E	15-30ft	15ft sq	pinky/white	10-12	5 or 10	B/C	S/T	z	Sd 2	Z6	N	4
Arctostaphylos															
manzanita	California	a	E	4-8ft	6-8ft sq	pinky/white	1-3	4 or 10	A/B	½Sh	z	Ctg 8-12 or Sd 2	Z6	J/S	4
Aster															
various	Europe	d	HP	6 in	1ft sq	lilac	9-11	4	B	S	—	Div 3	Z5	N	4
Azara															
microphylla	Chile	a	E	6-10ft	10ft sq	yellow	2-3	3-5	A/B/D	S	z	Ctg 9 or Lyg 10	Z6	M/Sh	1
Bergenia															
various	Siberia, China, Himalayas	d	HP	1-2ft	2ft sq	pinks & white	2-3 & 11	10 & 4	B	S/Sh	—	Div 4	Z6	F	4 & 2
Buddleia															
auriculata	South Africa	b	E	10ft	10ft sq	cream	9-1	4	A/B	S/T	y	Sd 2	Z6	D/S	1
Calluna															
vulgaris 'H.E. Beale'	Europe	b	E	2ft	2ft sq	pink	7-11	4 & 9	A/B	½S/Sh	y	Ctg 5	Z5	Sh	4
Camellia															
sasanqua	Japan	b	E	4-15ft	4-12ft sq	white to red	12-1	4 & 9	A/B	S/T	z	Ctg 5 or Sd 2	Z 6/7	D/F/T/Sh	2
japonica	Japan & China	b	E	4-30ft	4-10ft sq	various	1-5	4 & 9	A/B	½Sh	z	Ctg 5	Z6	J/T/Sh	4
X williamsii	garden hybrid	b	E	10ft	6ft sq	white & pinks	11-5	4 & 9	A/B	½Sh	z	Ctg 5	Z6	F/T	4
Ceanothus															
arboreus	California	a	E	8-20ft	5-20ft sq	blue	4-12	4	B/D	S/T	y/x	Ctg 7	Z 6/7	N/T	3

125

1	2	3	4	5	6	7	8	9	10	11	12	13	14	15	16
Ceratostigma willmottianum	China	b	D	2 ft	2 ft sq	blue	8-11	4	A/B	S/½T	x	Ctg 7	Z 6	N	4
Chaenomeles various	Japan	b	D	3-9 ft	8 ft sq	various	1-5	9-10	B	S/Sh	x/y	Ctg 7	Z 5	J/F/M/Sh	4
Chimonanthus praecox	China	b	D	6-10 ft	8 ft sq	yellow & purple	11-2	4 or 10	B	S	z	Lyg 5 or Sd 2	Z 6	D/J/F/S	1
Chionodoxa luciliae	Asia Minor	e	H	4 in	2 in sq	blue/white/pink	3-4	9/10	B	S/½Sh	—	Div 6	Z 5	M	4
Cistus × *pulverulentus*	Mediterranean	b	E	2 ft	3 ft sq	cerise	5-12	4	B/C	S/½T	y	Ctg 7	Z 6	D	3
Clematis cirrhosa	Mediterranean	c	E	8 ft	8 ft sq	cream	1-3	4 or 9	B/D	S/½Sh	z	Sd 6	Z 6	J/S	4
calycina (*balearica*)	Balearic Islands	c	E	10 ft	8 ft sq	green	9-3	4 or 9	B/D	S/½Sh/T	z	Sd 6	Z 6	J/F	4
Colchicum various	Asia Minor	e	P	2-8 in	8 in sq	white & pinks	10-3	6-8	B/D	S/½Sh	—	Sd 5	Z 5	N/J	4
Colletia cruciata	Uruguay	e	D	8 ft	8 ft sq	white	9-2	4	B	S	y	Ctg 5	Z 6	N	2
Cornus mas	S. Europe	a/b	D	20 ft	10-15 ft sq	yellow	2	10 or 3	B	S	y	Sd 10	Z 5	F	4
Coronilla glauca	S. Europe	b	E	8 ft	4 ft sq	yellow	1-12	4 & 10	B	S/T	y	Ctg 7	Z 6/7	N/J/T/S	2
Correa backhousiana	Tasmania	b	E	8 ft	4 ft sq	yellow-green	1-2	4	A/B	S/T	z	Ctg 7	Z 7	J/T	4
Cortaderia selloana	Argentina	d	HP	8-10 ft	5 ft sq	cream	10-12	3-4	B/D	S	x	Div 4	Z 6	D	4
Corylopsis pauciflora	Japan	b	D	4 ft	3 ft sq	yellow	2-3	4 or 9	A	S/½Sh	z	Lyg 3	Z 5/6	F	2
spicata	Japan	b	D	6 ft	7 ft sq	yellow	2-3	4 or 9	A/B	S/½Sh	z	Ctg 7	Z 5/6	F	2
Corylus avellana 'Contorta'	Europe	a/b	D	9 ft	6 ft sq	yellow	1-2	11	C	S	x	Suckers	Z 5	J	4
Crocus various	S. Europe & Asia Minor	e	P	2-4 in	4 in sq	various	11-3	4	B/D	S	—	Div 6	Z 5	N/D/J/F/M	4 & 2
Cyclamen various	Mediterranean	e	P	3-6 in	8 in sq	pinks & white	11-3	8	C/D	½Sh	—	Sd 4-6	Z 5/6	N/D/F/M/T	4 & 1
Cytisus nigricans	Europe to Russia	b	D	3 ft	3 ft sq	yellow	7-11	4	B/D	S	y	Ctg 6 & Sd 2	Z 5/6	S	4
Daboecia cantabrica	N. Spain	b	E	1½ ft	1½ ft sq	white & magenta	6-11	4 & 10	A	S/Sh	y	Ctg 6	Z 5	S	4

1	2	3	4	5	6	7	8	9	10	11	12	13	14	15	16
Daphne															
blagayana	S.E. Europe	b	E	9 in	3 ft sq	cream	3	4 & 10	C/D	S/½Sh	z	Div 8	Z5	M/Sh	1
laureola	Europe	b	E	3 ft	4 ft sq	yellow-green	2-3	4 & 10	C/D	Sh	z	Ctg 7	Z5	F/Sh	1
mezereum	Europe	b	D	2 ft+	2 ft sq	white & purple	2-3	10-4	B/D	S/½Sh	y	Sd 2	Z5	F/M	1
odora 'Aureomarginata'	China & Japan	b	E	3 ft+	2 ft sq	purple	2-4	10 & 4	B/D	S/½Sh	z	Ctg 6	Z6	F/M	1
Eccremocarpus															
scaber	Chile	c	D	10-20 ft	Indefinite	orange	6-11	4	B/D	S/T	y	Sd 2	Z 6/7	N/T	4
Edgeworthia															
chrysantha (papyrifera)	Himalayas & China	b	D	5-6 ft	5 ft sq	yellow	2-3	4-5	B	S/½Sh/T	z	Ctg 6	Z6	M	1
Eranthis															
various	Europe & Turkey	e	P	3 in	3 in sq	yellow	1-3	3	B/D	S/½Sh	—	Sd 9	Z5	J	4
Erica															
arborea 'Alpina'	Spain	b	E	5-8 ft	6-9 ft sq	white	2-3	4 & 9	A/B	S	y	Ctg 6	Z6	F	1
carnea	Europe	b	E	9-12 in	1½ ft sq	white/pinks	12-3	4 & 9	B	S	y/x	Ctg 6	Z6	F/M/S	4
Eriobotrya															
japonica 'Loquat'	China & Japan	a/b	E	10-30 ft	10 ft sq	cream	11-4	4	B/D	S/T	z	Sd 7	Z6	S	1
Erythronium															
various	Europe Asia & USA	e	P	6-9 in	6 in sq	various	4-5	9	A/B	½Sh	z	Sd 7	Z5	M	4
Escallonia															
'Iveyi'	South America	b	E	6 ft+	8 ft sq	white	6-11	3-4	B/D	S/½T	x	Ctg 7	Z6	N	2
Eucryphia															
× intermedia	Chile & Tasmania	a	E	12-15 ft	12 ft sq	white	8-12	3-4	A/B	S/½Sh	z	Ctg 8	Z6	N/Sh	2
Forsythia															
giraldiana	Yunnan	b	D	6-8 ft	8 ft sq	pale yellow	2-3	4 or 9	B	S/½Sh	y	Ctg 7	Z5	M	3
ovata	Korea	b	D	4-5 ft	4-6 ft sq	chrome	2-3	4 or 9	B	S/½Sh	y	Ctg 7	Z5	M	3
Fritillaria															
various	Europe USA & USSR	e	P	6-10 in	3 in sq	various	2-3	4 or 9	A/D	S/½Sh	—	Scales 8	Z5	M	4
Galanthus															
various	Asia Minor Europe & USSR	e	P	4-10 in	3-8 in sq	white	11-3	immed. af. fl.	B/D	S/½Sh	—	Div immed. af. fl.	Z5	N/D/J/F/Sh	3
Garrya															
elliptica	California Oregon	a/b	E	6-12 ft	9 ft sq	grey-green	1-2	5-6	B/D	½S/Sh/ ½T	y	Ctg 8 / Sd 2	Z7	J	4
Gazania															
× splendens	South Africa	d	E/P	4 in	1 ft sq	orange	5-12+	4 & 9	B/D	S/T	z	Ctg 9	Z7	D	4
Genista															
tinctoria	Europe	b	D	1 ft	3 ft sq	yellow	6-11	4	B/D	S	y	Sd 2 / Ctg 4	Z6	S	4
Gentiana															
acaulis	Europe	d	P	4 in	1 ft sq	deep blue	3-6	9	C/D	S	—	Div 6	Z5	Sh	4
sino-ornata	Western China	d	P	6 in	1 ft sq	royal blue & white	9-11	3-4	A/D	S/½Sh	—	Div 2	Z5	N/Sh	4

1	2	3	4	5	6	7	8	9	10	11	12	13	14	15	16
Grevillea															
alpina	South Australia	b	E	1 ft	1 ft sq	red & cream	1-12	4 & 9	A	S/T	z	Ctg 7	Z 6/7	N/T	4
rosmarinifolia	New South Wales	b	E	5 ft	6 ft sq	deep pink	1-8	4 & 9	A	S/T	z	Ctg 7	Z 6/7	T	4
Hamamelis															
various	China, Japan & USA	b	D	6-25 ft	6-25 ft sq	coppers & yellows	9-3	10 & 3	A/B	S/½Sh	z	Sd 2 or Gr 3	Z 5	D/J	1 & 3
Hebe															
'Autumn Glory'	New Zealand	b	E	1-3 ft	2-3 ft sq	violet	8-12	4 & 9	B/D	S	y	Ctg 5	Z 6/7	N	4
speciosa hybrids	New Zealand	b	E	5 ft	5 ft sq	pinks & purples	7-12	4 & 9	B/D	S/T	y	Ctg 7	Z 7	N/T	4
Helleborus															
various	Europe, W. Asia & Medit.	b/d	E/H	1-2 ft	1-2 ft sq	various	12-5	4 & 9	B/D	S/½Sh/Sh	—	Sd 2 & 8 / Div 4	Z 5/6	J/F/M/Sh	4 & 3
Hepatica															
nobilis	Europe	d	P	4-6 in	1 ft sq	white, blues & pinks	2-4	4 & 9	B/C/D	½Sh	x	Div 9	Z 5	M/Sh	4
Hypericum															
calycinum	Europe & Asia	b	E	1½ ft	Indef. Invasive	yellow	7-11	4	B/D	S/Sh	x	Ctg 4	Z 6	Sh	4
Ipheion															
uniflorum	South America	e	P	6 in	6 in sq	white & blues	2-5	5	B	S/½Sh	—	Div 5	Z 6	M	3
Iris															
bakeriana	Asia Minor	e	P	1½ ft	½ ft sq	ultramarine	1-2	7-9	B/D	S	—	Div 6	Z 5	J	2
danfordiae	Turkey	e	P	3 in	3 in sq	yellow	1-2	7-9	B/D	S	—	Div 5	Z 5	F	2
histrioides 'Major'	Turkey	e	P	4 in	3 in sq	royal blue	1-2	7-9	C/D	S	—	Div 6	Z 5	J	3
reticulata	Caucasus	e	P	6-9 in	3 in sq	blues & mauves	2-3	8-10	B/D	S/½Sh	—	Div 6	Z 5	F/Sh	1
unguicularis	Algeria	e	P	1¼ ft	1 ft sq	& white	9-4	4 & 9	B/D	S/½Sh	—	Div 4	Z 6	F/S	3
Jasminum															
nudiflorum	China	b	D	15 ft	Indef.	yellow	11-3	10-4	B	S	x	Ctg 8	Z 6	N/F/M/T	4
primulinum (mesnyi)	Yunnan	c	E	8 ft	Indef.	yellow	3-5	4-5	B	S/T	y	Ctg 8	Z 7	F/M/T	4
Lardizabala															
biternata	Chile	c	E	25 ft	Indef.	purple & white	11-3	5	B/D	S/½Sh/T	y	Sd 4 & Ctg 7-8	Z 7	T/S	4
Lavatera															
olbia 'Rosea'	Southern France	b	D	5-10 ft	6 ft sq	pink	7-11	4	B/D	S	x	Sd 2	Z 6	D/T	4
Leucojum (Snowflake)															
various	Europe & Mediterranean	e	P	4-10 in	2-8 in sq	white or pink	8-5	5	B	S/T or ½Sh	—	Div or Sd 2 or 5	Z 7	M/T/Sh	2
Lithospermum															
rosmarinifolium	Southern Italy	b	E	15 in	1 ft sq	bright blue	1-2	4	B/D	S/T	z	Ctg 3	Z 6/7	F/T	4
Lonicera															
fragrantissima	China	b	½E	4-6 ft	4-6 ft sq	cream	12-2	10-3	B	S	y	Ctg 7	Z 5	D/S	1
Magnolia															
campbellii	Himalayas	a	D	to 60 ft	Indef.	pink or white	2	5 & 9	A	S/½Sh/T	z	Lyg 5 or	Z 5	F	3
stellata	Japan	a/b	D	5-10 ft	5-10 ft sq		3-4	5 & 9	A/B	S/½Sh	z	Ctg 6	Z 5	M	2
Mahonia															
various	China & Burma	b	E	6 ft	6 ft sq	yellows	11-3	4 & 9	B	S & S/T	y	Lyg 7	Z 6	N/F/M	1 & 3

128

1	2	3	4	5	6	7	8	9	10	11	12	13	14	15	16
Mesembryanthemum deltoides	South Africa	d	EP	to 9 in	Indef.	various	7-11	5	B/D	S/T	z	Ctg 8	Z6	J	4
Muscari various	Mediterranean & Asia Minor	e	P	4-6 in	2-3 in sq	whites & blues	3-4	6-8	B	S/½Sh	—	Div 6	Z5	M/Sh	4 & 2
Myrtus communis tarentina	Mediterranean	b	E	3-6 ft	6ft sq	cream	7-11	5	B/D	S/½T	y	Ctg 7	Z6	N	1
Narcissus various	around Mediteranean	e	P	3-12 in	2-3 in sq	white & yellow	11-4	9-10	B	S/½Sh	—	Sd 2 & 9	Z5/6	F/M	3
Nerine bowdenii	South Africa	e	P	1½ ft	1 ft sq	pink	9-11	8	B/D	S/T	—	Div 8	Z6	N/S	4
Osmanthus various	Japan Himalayas & China	b	E	4-8 ft	3-6 ft sq	white or cream	9-3	4 & 9	B	S/½Sh	y	Ctg 7-8	Z6	N/D/M	1
Osmaronia (Nuttallia) cerasiformis	California	b	D	6-8 ft	6-8 ft sq	cream	2-3	10-3	B	S/½Sh	y	Ctg 7 or Div 10 or 2	Z6	M	2
Parrotia (Iron Tree) *persica*	Iran & Caucasus	a	D	20 ft	to 40 ft sq	stamens crimson	1-3	10-3	B/C/D	S/½Sh	x on wall or z	Lyg 9	Z5	M	4
Petasites fragrans	Mediterranean	d	P	1 ft	6 ft sq	lilac	1-2	4	B	Sh/½T	—	Sd 5-6 Root Ctgs 10 or 3	Z6	J	1
Pieris japonica 'Xmas Cheer'	Japan	b	E	5-10 ft	5-7 ft sq	pinky/white	3-4	4 & 9	A/B	½Sh/½T	y	Ctg 8	Z5/6	M	3
Primula various	Himalayas Caucasus & Europe	d	P	2-9 in	4-18 in sq	various	1-3	4	A/B or C D or Wet	½Sh	—	Sd 5, Div 7 or 9 or Ctg 8	Z5	J/F/M/T/Sh	2 & 4
Prunus davidiana	China	a	D	12-20ft	8-16 ft sq	pink &	1-2	10-3	B	S/½T	y	Budding	Z6	J	3
incisa	Japan	a/b	D	8-10ft	8-10ft sq	white	1-2	10-3	B	S	y	Lyg 7	Z6	J	3
subhirtella 'Autumnalis'	Japan	a	D	20-30ft	20-30 ft sq	pinky/white	11-4	10-3	B	S	y	Ctg 7	Z6	N/F/M/S	3
Pulmonaria various	Europe	d	E	6-15 in	15 in sq	white, blue & pink	2-4	4 & 9	B	S or Sh	—	Div 9	Z5	M	4
Puschkinia scilloides	Lebanon	e	P	6in	3 in sq	bluish/white	3-4	9/10	B	S	—	Div 7	Z5	M	4
Ranunculus calandrinioides	North Africa	d	P	6in	12 in sq	white or pink	2-3	5	B	S/½Sh/T	—	Div 8	Z7	M/T	4
Rhododendron various	many areas	a/b	E/D	2-25 ft	4-25 ft sq	white, red, yellow & pinks	12-3	9	A	½Sh	y	Sd 2 Ctg 7	Z6	D/J/F/M	1 & 4
Romulea bulbocodium	Southern Europe	e	P	2-3 in	3 in sq	mauve	3-4	5	B/D	S/T	—	Div 5	Z7	T	4

129

1	2	3	4	5	6	7	8	9	10	11	12	13	14	15	16
Rosa various	many areas	b/c	D	4-25 ft	4-25 ft sq	whites & pinks	6-12	3 & 9	B/C/D	S/½Sh	x/y	Ctg 10	Z6	N/S/Sh	1 & 4
Salvia rutilans	Mexico	b	E	2-4ft	3 ft sq	scarlet	6-12	5	B/D	S/T	y	Ctg 7	Z7	N	2
Sarcococca various	China	b	E	1-3ft	1½-4 ft sq	creamy/white	1-3	10	B	Sh	y	Sd 10	Z5	F/Sh	1 & 3
Saxifraga various	European Alps	d	E	2-6in	6-8 in sq	purple, yellow white & pink	1-3	4 & 9	C/D	S or ½Sh	—	Ctg or Div 5	Z6	M/T	4
Schizostylis coccinea	South Africa	e	P	2 ft	½ ft sq	red or pinks	10-12	4	B	S	—	Div 6	Z6	N/D	4
Scilla various	Iran, Siberia & Southern Europe	e	P	3-8 in	4 in sq	white blues & pinks	2-4	9-11	B/C/D	S/½Sh	—	Div 6	Z5	M	4
Spartium junceum	Spain & Mediterranean	e	D	5-10 ft	5-10 ft sq	yellow	6-11	4	B/D	S	x	Sd 2	Z6	S	2
Stachyurus praecox	Japan	a/b	D	6-8 ft	6-7 ft sq	pale yellow	2-3	10-3	A/B	S/½Sh	y	Ctg 7	Z6	F	4
Sternbergia various	Asia Minor	e	P	6-12 in	4 in sq	yellow	9-11 or 2-3	4 or 7-8	C/D or B/D	S	—	Div 6 or Div 7	Z6	N/M	4
Sycopsis sinensis	Central China	b	E	5-8 ft	5-8 ft sq	orange	2-3	4 & 9	A/B	½Sh	y	Ctg 7	Z5	F	3
Tecophilaea cyanocrocus	Chile	e	P	3 in	3 in sq	blues & violet	2-3	5	A/B/D	S/T	—	Div 7	Z6	M	4
Tulipa kaufmanniana	Central Asia	e	P	8 in	6 in sq	reds & creams	2-3	11	C/D	S	—	Sd 9	Z5	F	4
pulchella	Iran & Turkey	e	P	5 in	3 in sq	pink & violet	2-3	11	C/D	S	—	Div 10	Z5	F	4
Ulex europaeus & gallii	Europe	b	E	1-5 ft	2-8 ft sq	yellow	3-5 & 7-11	9-4	A/B/C/D	S	x	Ctg 7-8	Z6	M	4
Viburnum various	Mediterranean & Himalayas, Korea & China	a/b	E/D	5-15 ft	5-10 ft sq	pink or white	11-3	10&4(E) 10-3(D)	B	S/½Sh	y	Ctg 7	Z6	N/D/J/F/Sh	1 & 3
Vinca difformis	Algeria & Mediterranean	d	E	4 in	3 ft sq	lilac/blue mauve	11-3	10-4	B	S/½Sh	x	Ctg 8	Z6	M/Sh	4
Viola various	Europe & Asia Minor	d	P	3-6 in	12-18 in sq	various	1-12	9 or 3	A/B/C	S/½Sh	—	Ctg or Div 9	Z6	D/M	1 & 3
Zauschneria californica	Mexico California	d or b	P or D	12 in	18 in sq	red	9-11	5	A/B/C/D	S/T	z	Ctg or Div 6	Z7	D	4

List of Gardens and Nurseries

I give below some of the gardens I know and have visited or have been recommended to, where winter-flowering plants are to be seen in all their stages of development. Many of the shrubs and trees are of very fine proportions and rather more than the average gardener can hope to aspire to, but nevertheless it is exciting to see some of these plants in their full flowering maturity. A great deal of pleasure can then be gained by looking for, finding the ideal situation and bringing to flower a young plant; and except for the great tree of the forest, *Magnolia campbellii*, which you do have to wait more than twenty years to see in bloom, the majority of plants flower in the first year, and so give instant joy and pleasure.

When you have seen the plant that interests you in the setting of a lovely garden, you can then check out the nursery which will provide the plant. Look for the kind of nursery, often quite a small one, where the owners raise their own stock and take a great interest in their plants, or are prepared to get something you require that they do not grow. The large garden centres are marvellous to visit, dazzling us with their display, but they very often keep to the well-known varieties of plant and do not carry the slightly more unusual stock, one of which may be the very plant you are seeking. And they have no means of dealing with an individual demand, so large is their turnover of popular lines.

However, if you cannot get a particular plant from a local nursery, always go to a colder area for your order, and then the plant should thrive after its tougher upbringing.

But the advantages of dealing with a good local nursery — if you can find one — are that you can go and choose your plants, and the soil that they have been grown in is more likely to approximate to the one in your own garden, as to type and temperature. Also the nursery owners will often be prepared to visit you and give advice as to the best plants which will thrive in your location, or suggest the best place for the positioning of a special plant you want them to provide. I have a good local camellia and rhodo-dendron nursery where they are extremely helpful in this way. And I'm sure these really caring nurserymen can be found in many areas, if they are assiduously tracked down. And it is often necessary to do this when buying some of the winter-flowering plants because, hardy as such plants can be, most people are not geared to flowers in the garden in winter.

NORTH AMERICAN GARDENS WHERE PLANTS MENTIONED IN THE BOOK CAN BE SEEN

Alabama
Birmingham Botanical Gardens
2612 Lane Park Road, Birmingham,
AL 35223

Rhododendron, Camellia, Cornus, Iris, Rosa

California
Regional Parks Botanic Garden
Tilden Regional Park, Berkeley, CA 94708

Ceanothus and Arctostaphylos

Descanso Gardens
1418 Descanso Drive, La Canada-Flintridge, CA 91011

Rhododendron, Rosa, Camellia, (largest collection in the world)

Colorado
Denver Botanic Gardens, Inc.
909 York Street, Denver, CO 80206

Iris, herb and rock gardens, alpine study area

Connecticut
The Connecticut Arboretum at
Connecticut College, New London
CT 06320

Rhododendron and 375 species of woody plants of 116 genera

Delaware
Winterthur Museum and Gardens
Winterthur, DE 19735

Rhododendron, Narcissus, Viburnum, Corylopsis

District of Columbia
US National Arboretum, 24th and R Streets
NE Washington, DC 20002

Camellia, Cornus, Iris, Magnolia, Narcissus, Prunus, Rhododendron, Viburnum

Florida
Harry P. Leu Botanical Garden, 1730 North
Forest Avenue, Orlando, FL 32803

Camellia, Rosa

Illinois
Chicago Horticultural Society Botanic
Garden, Lake Cook Road, Box 400
Glencoe, IL 60022

Alpines, herbs, perennials, Ericaceae, Narcissus

Indiana

The Holcomb Garden, Department of
Botany, Butler University
4600 Sunset Avenue, Indianapolis
IN 46208

600 trees, many flowering shrubs,
bulbs, perennials

Maine

Thuya Garden, Asticou Terraces,
Paul Favour, Trustee Northeast Harbor
ME 04662

Rhododendron, Trees and Shrubs,
English garden of annuals and
perennials

Massachusetts

Alexandria Botanical Gardens and
Hunnewell Arboretum, Wellesley
College, Wellesley, MA 02181

Rhododendron, Viburnum,
greenhouses of different climatic
regions; over 1,000 species and
cultivars

Michigan

Matthaei Botanical Gardens
The University of Michigan
1800 North Dixboro Road,
Ann Arbor, MI 48105

Temperate and native plants

Dow Gardens, 1018 West Main Street
Midland, MI 48640

Cornus Hamamelis, Magnolia,
Rhododendron, Viburnum

Missouri

Missouri Botanical Garden, 2101 Tower
Grove Avenue, St Louis, MO

Greenhouse of 4 basic climate
zones, English woodland and
scented garden.

Mississippi

Beauvoir, The Jefferson Davis Shrine
U.S. Highway 90, Biloxi, MS

Special plant collections

New York

The New York Botanical Garden
Bronx, NY 10458

Seasonal displays

Brooklyn Botanic Garden
1000 Washington Avenue, Brooklyn
NY 11225

Forsythia, Hamamelis, Prunus,
Rhododendron, Viburnum,
13 specialised gardens

George Landis Arboretum, Esperance
NY 12066

Rhododendron and program
testing effects of winter conditions
on exotic species

Pennsylvania

The Gardens at the Ambler Campus of
Temple University, Ambler, PA 19002

800 species and cultivars of woody
plants and dwarf shrubs

Longwood Gardens, Inc., Kennett Square PA 19348	Rock and heather gardens, rare shrubs & specimen trees. Seasonal displays.
Morris Arboretum of the University of Pennsylvania, 9414 Meadowbrook Avenue, Philadelphia, PA 19118	Magnolia slope, Viburnum, Hamamelis, Prunus, E.H. Wilson collections.

Maryland

London Town Publik House and Gardens 839 London Town Road, Edgewater MD 21037	Camellias sasanqua, japonica and oleifera. Magnolia, Viburnum and winter garden

Estate Gardens

New York

Sonnenberg Gardens and Mansion 151 Charlotte Street, Canandaigua NY 14424	9 designed gardens including pansy, rose, rock. Specimen trees.

North Carolina

Biltmore House and Gardens, Asheville NC 28803	Rhododendron, Magnolia, Rosa, 4-acre walled English garden

GARDENS OPEN THROUGH THE WINTER

ENGLAND

Berkshire
Savill Garden, Windsor Great Park
Valley Gardens, Windsor Great Park

Cambridgeshire
University Botanic Garden, Cambridge

Cheshire
Ness Gardens, Wirral

Cornwall
Lanhydrock, nr Bodmin
Mount Edgcumbe, nr Plymouth

Devon
Marwood Hill, nr Barnstaple
Overbecks Garden, Sharpitor, Salcombe
Saltram House, Plymouth
Torre Abbey, Torquay

Dorset
Abbotsbury Sub-Tropical Gardens, Abbotsbury,
nr Weymouth

Essex
Beth Chatto Gardens, Elmstead Market

Gloucestershire
Barnsley House Garden, Barnsley, nr Cirencester

Hampshire
Furzey Gardens, Minstead, nr Lyndhurst
Macpenny's, Bransgore, nr Christchurch

Hereford & Worcester
The Commandery, Sidbury, Worcester
Dinmore Manor, nr Hereford

Hertfordshire
Capel Manor, nr Enfield

Humberside
Sewerby Hall, Bridlington

Kent
Owl House Gardens, Lamberhurst
Port Lympne Gardens, Lympne, Hythe

London
Chiswick House Garden, Chiswick
Hall Place, Bexley
Ham House Garden, Richmond
Kew Gardens, Kew (Royal Botanic Gardens)

Northumberland
Wallington Garden, Cambo

Nottinghamshire
Newstead Abbey, Linby

Oxfordshire
Botanic Gardens, Oxford
Waterperry Gardens, nr Wheatley

Somerset
Clapton Court, Crewkerne
Hadspen House, Castle Cary

Staffordshire
Shugsborough, Stafford

Surrey
Claremont Landscape Garden, Esher
Winkworth Arboretum, nr Godalming

East Sussex
Beeches Farm, nr Uckfield
The Spring Hill Wildfowl Park, Forest Row

West Sussex
Wakehurst Place Garden, nr Ardingly

Wiltshire
Luckington Court, Luckington

West Yorkshire
Harlow Car Gardens, Harrogate
Lotherton Hall, Aberford

IRELAND

Johnstown Castle, Wexford
National Botanic Gardens, Glasnevin, Dublin 9

SCOTLAND

Dumfries & Galloway
Threave Garden, nr Castle Douglas

Grampian Region
Crathes Castle Gardens, Banchory

Highlands Region
Inverewe, Poolewe, Wester Ross

Lothian Region
Inveresk Lodge, Inveresk
Royal Botanic Garden, Edinburgh

Strathclyde Region
Achamore Gardens, Isle of Gigha
Balloch Castle Country Park, Balloch
Botanic Gardens, Glasgow
Brodick Castle Garden, Isle of Arran
Greenbank Garden, Glasgow
Ross Hall Park, Glasgow
Torosay Castle Gardens, Craignure, Isle of Mull

Four college gardens of the University of Oxford with a good display of winter flowers

Merton College, Merton Street
New College, New College Lane
St John's College, St Giles
Wadham College, Parks Road

NURSERIES

Great Britain

Ashby & Son, Woodcote, Oxfordshire	General plants, trees & shrubs
David Austin Roses, Bowling Green Lane, Albrighton, Wolverhampton WV7 3HB	Roses, plants and iris
Avon Bulbs, Bathford, Bath BA1 8ED	Rare and uncommon bulbs
Walter Blom & Son, Ltd, Coombelands Nurseries, Leavesden, Watford, Herts WD2 7BH	Bulbs and plants
Bodnant Garden Nursery, Tal-y-Cafn, Colwyn Bay, Clwyd LL28 5RE	Trees and shrubs
Bressingham Gardens, Diss Norfolk IP22 2AB	General plants
Fairlight Camellia Nursery, Three Oaks, Guestling, East Sussex	Camellias and rhododendrons
Filsham Nurseries, Charles Road West, St Leonards-on-Sea, East Sussex	Trees, shrubs and heathers
Fisk's Clematis Nursery, Westleton, nr Saxmundham, Suffolk IP17 3AJ	Clematis
Great Dixter Nurseries, Northiam,. East Sussex	Clematis and other shrubs and plants
Hilliers Nurseries (Winchester) Ltd, Ampfield House, Ampfield, nr Romsey, Hants.	Trees and shrubs
Hollington Nurseries, Woolton Hill, Newbury, Berks RG15 9XT	Herbs and other small plants
C.J. Marchant, Keeper's Hill Nursery, Stapehill, nr Wimborne, Dorset	Trees and shrubs
Murrells Nursery, Broomer's Hill Lane, Pulborough, West Sussex	Trees and shrubs
Chiltern Seeds, Bortree Stile, Ulverston, Cumbria LA12 7PB	Large range of seeds
Thompson and Morgan, London Road, Ipswich, Suffolk IP2 0BA	Large range of seeds

North America

W. Atlee Burpee Co., Parks Avenue, Warminster, Pennsylvania 18974	Seeds
Geo. W. Park Seed Co., Greenwood, South Carolina 29647	Seeds
Stokes Seed Inc., Main Street, Box 548, Buffalo, New York 14240	Seeds
Thompson & Morgan, PO Box 100, Farmingdale, New Jersey 07727	Seeds
Wayside Gardens Co., Hodges, South Carolina 29645	Plants
White Flower Farm, Litchfield, Connecticut 06759	Plants

North American Societies

American Camellia Society,
Box 1217, Fort Valley, GA 31030

American Iris Society,
6518 Beachy Avenue, Wichita, KS 67206

American Magnolia Society
Box 129, Nanuet, NY 10954

The American Rhododendron Society,
14635 S.W. Bull Mountain Road, Tigard, OR 97223

American Rose Society,
Box 30,000, Shreveport, LA 71130

Hardy Plant Society,
Pacific Northwest Group, 124 N. 181st Street,
Seattle, Washington 98133.

American Rock Garden Society,
Norman Singer, Norfolk Road,
S. Sandisfield, Massachusetts 01255

Appendix II

Conversion Tables

Fahrenheit — Celsius

°F	°C
−58	−50
23	− 5
32	0
41	5
50	10
59	15
68	20

Imperial — Metric

Imperial	Metric
1 in	2.5 cm
6 in	15 cm
1 ft	30 cm
3 ft	91 cm
10 ft	3 m
20 ft	6 m
30 ft	9 m
60 ft	18 m

Maps

Hardiness Zones of North America and Europe

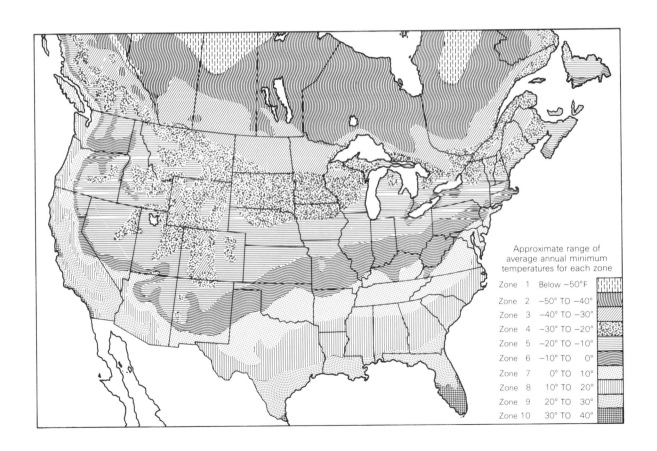

Approximate range of
average annual minimum
temperatures for each zone

Zone 1   Below −50°F

Zone 2   −50° TO −40°

Zone 3   −40° TO −30°

Zone 4   −30° TO −20°

Zone 5   −20° TO −10°

Zone 6   −10° TO   0°

Zone 7   0° TO   10°

Zone 8   10° TO   20°

Zone 9   20° TO   30°

Zone 10   30° TO   40°

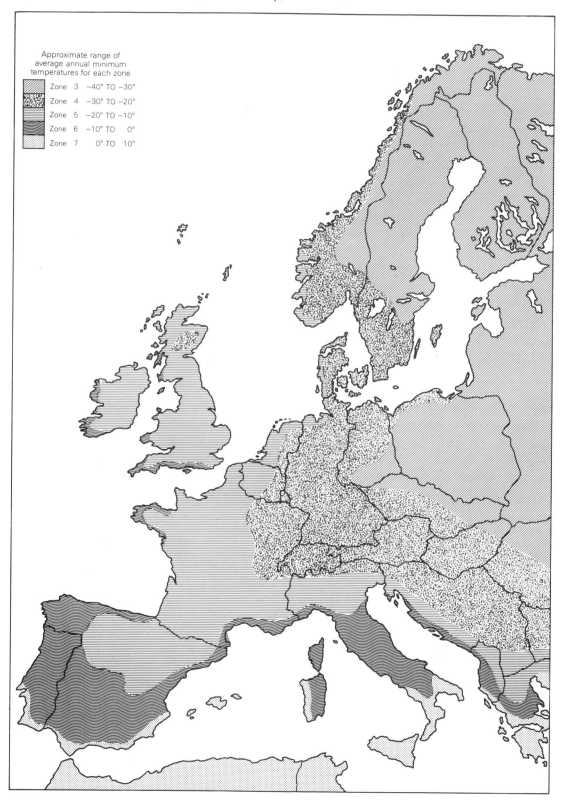

Approximate range of
average annual minimum
temperatures for each zone

	Zone 3	−40° TO −30°
	Zone 4	−30° TO −20°
	Zone 5	−20° TO −10°
	Zone 6	−10° TO 0°
	Zone 7	0° TO 10°

Index